THE POWER
TO HEAL

*A você a mensagem de amor da casa de
Dom Inácio desejando que os benfeitores
espirituais o ilumine e ampare.*

João Teixeira de Faria
PRESIDENTE DA CASA DE DOM INÁCIO

THE POWER TO HEAL

*A clear, concise
and comprehensive guide
to Energy Healing*

Robert Pellegrino-Estrich

This book was printed in the United States of America and in Brazil

To order additional copies of this book, contact:

Robert Pellegrino Estrich
Rua Servidão, Qd. 20, lt. 05
Abadiânia – Goiás – Brazil. CEP 72940-000
E-mail: robertestrich@gmail.com
Tel.: + 55 62 92224119

CONTENTS

PART TWO

SPIRITUAL HEALING

Dedicated to all those divinely gifted
healing mediums, who silently devote their lives
to unstinting spiritual guidance and the
easing of suffering of their fellowman.
Dedicated healers, such as my ex-wife Caterina and
Joao Teixeira da Faria, to whom I owe much in
personal health and spiritual enlightenment.

FOREWORD

Millions of people worldwide are seeking complimentary health protocols. In the U.S.A in 1997 alone, more than 83 million Americans consulted complimentary and alternative health practitioners.

It is estimated that visits to complimentary care practitioners in the US exceed those to primary care physicians by more than 200 million visits per year! A conservative estimate by the National Center for Complimentary and Alternative Medicine (NCCAM) suggests that, in 1997, Americans spent 21.2 billion dollars on complimentary and alternative health care. It is now estimated that 42% of the U.S. population use complimentary medical therapies.

The results of a 1998 American survey, conducted to establish why people seek alternative therapies, were published in the Journal of the American Medical Association. The study revealed that people are desirous of *"treating illness within a larger context of spiritual and life meaning . . . the use of alternative care is part of a broader value orientation and set of cultural beliefs, one that embraces a holistic, spiritual orientation to life."*[1] Most of these do not want to replace conventional medicine; they want to complement it with other treatments.

Spiritual healing is a time-honoured form of complimentary therapy. It can be traced back beyond 1500 BC and, in modern times, has stood the test of many scientific examinations. Now this age-old method is undergoing a popular revival. Whilst some fraudulent practitioners encourage ridicule, the majority of "gifted" spiritual healers are dedicated and compassionate therapists. But, in this age of certification, having a natural propensity to heal is not sufficient. This book is designed to guide and encourage those who feel they have this "propensity" with facts, supportive evidence and practical techniques towards effective use of their "gift".

This book is unlike any other energy-healing book—it considers all forms of popular energy healing modalities, examines them and then selects the core principals that are common to all. It discards the rhetoric and condenses the essential ingredients to a single effective method. It is frank, concise and takes a direct and honest approach to man's oldest healing procedure—*the laying-on-of-hands*, now referred to as *spiritual healing*.

Many people feel they have the natural propensity to heal but lack the time or finances to pursue lengthy courses. They want information and guidance in a more concise and expeditious way to speed them through the necessary steps towards implementing their healing abilities. *The Power to Heal* serves these needs.

For anyone who feels they have the seeds of the healing gift it will offer them encouragement, knowledge and specifics to commence healing—professionally or as a part time interest. We do not subscribe to any commercial or divergent teachings that cloud the simple truths of compassionate healing. We believe there is but one truth and one source. Any modality that claims exclusivity is just a diversion from the simple truth; human beings have a divine ability to heal each other with universal energies supplied by God through spirit guides in the ethereal world. Use this knowledge with love and true compassion to heal or sooth your fellow human and in return you will be blessed with spiritual rewards beyond your widest expectations.

The Power to Heal has been compiled from my participation and observations whilst assisting my wife Caterina (a gifted healer with twenty-five years of experience), from the content of my seminars on healing and mediumship and my many years of close association with Joao de Deus, Brazil's most powerful and effective healer about whom my book—*The Miracle Man*—is written.

We have explored and cross-referenced a wide spectrum of research with our own personal knowledge and experiences, recorded in our clinic records. We have avoided the mythical, substantiated the truth, proved the difficult-to-believe and confirmed the results. Wherever possible, we have endeavoured to substantiate our findings with supporting evidence and true case studies.

NOTE:

The contents of this book are not meant to replace the advice of a physician. Any person with an illness, mental or physical, should be aware of the value of seeking a variety of opinions in deciding a course of treatment. No healer, physician or alternative practitioner is perfect. A person seeking healing should use his or her best judgement in deciding the most suitable treatment protocol for them.

INTRODUCTION

W e are energy beings. We are, in fact, three bodies in one; a physical body, a spiritual body and an energy body, each motivated and influenced by emotional and mental faculties of the heart and the mind, intertwined and interdependent one upon the other. Current medical procedures treat only one—the physical. But let us consider this simple question; if so called modern medicine, in its current scientific form, began less than 500 years ago, what did mankind do to correct disease during the past two million years of evolution? This is not to trivialize the enormous advances made in modern medicine but, in our enthusiasm to embrace mankind's scientific sophistication, we have discarded our own God-given methods to heal the body complete.

Dis-ease occurs in any one of the three bodies. Most often it begins in the human energy fields. It is logical that most cures lie there also.

Bio-energy Healing, often called magnetic or energy healing, is acceptable to most people because it complies with accepted scientific knowledge. *Part One* of this book explores the proof and effectiveness of this method. Thousands of scientific experiments and theories from Paracelcius to Dr Lieberman provide irrefutable evidence for anyone who seeks it. It is demonstrable, logical, scientific and verifiable. In addition, energy healing is safe and has none of the side effects that often accompany allopathic drug use.

Spiritual Healing is a little more mystifying; "If healing is a gift", the purists will say, "How can it be taught?" There is much truth in this—there are some aspects that cannot be taught—we cannot give a person "the gift". Most humans, however, have some ability to heal, of course there are many who have a greater propensity than others and there are those who seem to have been bestowed with a powerful healing gift indeed. The purpose of this book is to provoke you to explore, learn and understand the possibilities of your "higher connection" and to establish some realistic basis on which to begin, some guidance to develop your inherent ability to heal.

For those who want to nurture and develop their natural healing talent, this book will enable them to recognize and awaken those hidden abilities. It will provide practical knowledge for a better appreciation of *Spiritual Healing* and how it works. It will explore both the fundamentals and the techniques to provide you with the confidence and the courage to pursue a healing path. It will, in addition, enlighten and open your mind, and connect you to the reality of your soul and the purpose for your existence.

In these times, when natural therapies are increasingly accepted by a wider proportion of the population, including many orthodox medical practitioners, this book will fill the need of alternative practitioners who wish to add that "extra dimension" to their practice by treating the core of the problem; the unseen *bio-energy* of the human body where a large proportion of dis-ease begins. A better diagnosis or healing is invariably achieved when the help and guidance of spirit guides are sought.

We have purposefully divided the book into two parts because we acknowledge there are those who choose to live by accepted beliefs and tangible realities. They may gain all they need from *Part One—Bio-Energies*, which deals with healing energies and their application. Many people do not embrace a full acceptance of spiritual beliefs. For them, *Part One—Bio-energies* will be most beneficial—providing proof of energy healing with tangible scientific evidence to support the theories.

Those who want to explore the aspects of Spiritual Healing in which energies are delivered by spirit guides, using the therapist as a channel, will find *Part Two—Spiritual Healing* most enlightening. It provides information on spirit attunement, energy transfer, spirit operations and the seldom-discussed problem of "attachments". It examines mediumship, reincarnation, multiple-dimension existence and psychic diagnostics. In addition it offers practical advice on setting up a healing clinic, therapist integrity, counselling, referrals and working with other practitioners.

There are sure to be aspects of this book that may be difficult for some to accept; time and practice will prove them not only real, but also invaluable. We will provide the evidence to substantiate what we say, but ultimately it may take time for these ideas to become part of your personal belief system.

It should be acknowledged that there are many degrees or levels of healing ability. There are higher levels that we may not achieve in this life. However, there is much good work to be done at all levels and all that can be expected of any practitioner is that they commit themselves sincerely to a compassionate desire to aid their fellow human.

Healing does not restrict itself to any race, religion, class or belief. All humanity has the right to explore the universal gift of healing with energies, without restrictions or taboos, and in so doing, enlighten themselves with the truth of our purpose in this wonderful time/space reality we call "life".

The connection to and utilization of universal energies is not only about healing. In its wider context it is about communication with those who guide us through this life. It's about knowledge from the universal records and the development of our true potential through living in the awareness of multiple realities of creation. It is, in fact, a way of life, more rewarding, more satisfying than you could ever imagine.

The Power to Heal
Is inherent in Man's ability
To connect to and transmit
Universal healing energies,
To use his body as a channel for healing guides
And his mind to direct them,
But it is GOD who heals,
The healer is only an attuned vessel.

PART ONE

BIO - ENERGY HEALING

CAN I BECOME
A HEALER?

- If you have a deep inner yearning to give of yourself to ease the suffering of the sick, to take away pain and stress.

- If you possess compassion and sympathy for those who are afflicted and if you are willing to sacrifice your time without pecuniary reward.

- If you are generous in nature and are willing to render service for good cause, you possess the spiritual qualities that mark the healing gift.

- This healing potential only then needs the development of attunement with the spirit source of healing, practice and the opportunity to give it practical expression.

Harry Edwards

CHAPTER ONE

HISTORICAL EVIDENCE OF
ENERGY HEALING

*"Various esoteric sources have long suggested that human beings are capable of healing one another by utilizing the special energy potentials, which are brought into each lifetime. This healing ability has had many names throughout the centuries, including laying-on-of-hands, healing, psychic healing, spiritual healing and therapeutic touch."*²

To be an effective healer you must have an unshakable confidence in what you do. Historic and scientific evidence will provide a basis for that self-assurance. Historically, records exist dating back beyond 3500 years suggesting that energy healing was used to relieve the ills of humanity even before recorded history. As well, there is an abundance of scientific evidence that verifies the effectiveness of energy healing to substantiate and cultivate that confidence.

In civilisations before recorded history, healing was performed by healer-priests, shamans, witchdoctors and tribal medicine men. Their roles in each of their societies may differ but their techniques were often remarkably similar, which suggests that they were utilizing the same healing forces. As long as man has existed there has been a belief that certain individuals could heal the sick by simply touching them, and there is a wealth of evidence of successful results, witnessed and documented, to substantiate that belief.

Historic evidence for the medical use of energy healing can be found recorded in the Ebers Papyrus of ancient Egypt, dated around 1552 BC. This document describes the laying-on-of-hands for medical treatment and reveals many case records. Four hundred years before Christ, it is recorded that the Greeks used a form of therapeutic touch in their temples for healing the sick. The writing of Aristophanes details the use of such therapies to restore a blind man's sight and to return fertility to a barren woman. Around 1200 BC another Greek physician named Aesculepius was so successful in healing the sick that the Greeks immortalised him as their god of medicine and built hundreds of temples to him where the sick could sleep in order to receive his healing powers.

Hippocrates, the father of modern medicine personally used the power of energy healing. At the turn of the fifth century BC he describes the same phenomenon as experienced, not only by himself, but also by his fellow doctors. The same application experienced by healers today:

> *"It is believed by experienced doctors that the heat which oozes out of the hand, on being applied to the sick, is highly salutary. It has often appeared while I have been soothing my patients, as if there was a singular property in my hands to pull and draw away from the affected parts, aches and diverse impurities, by*

laying my hand upon the place, and by extending my
fingers towards it. Thus it is known to some of the
learned that health may be implanted in the sick by
certain gestures and by contact, (just) as some diseases
may be communicated from one to another.[5]

It is paradoxical that the medical establishment considers Hippocrates to be the founder of modern medicine. Upon graduation doctors take the Hippocratic oath, and yet the majority of medical professionals ignore the evidence of energy healing. There are of course many who do believe and even apply energy healing to their daily practice, albeit secretly or in the simple guise of their religious beliefs—by prayer to God.

The Bible has many references to the laying-on-of-hands for both medical and spiritual maladies. It is well known that the miraculous healings of Jesus were achieved by this method. The teachings of Jesus stated quite clearly that anyone was capable of this method of healing; *"these things that I do, so can ye do and more."* This is a profound statement by a man who influenced the course of humanity more than any other in recorded history and is credited with the ultimate in healing ability. This statement is recorded in the world's most read book—the Bible—and yet it is passed over without due consideration. What he said is profound; he said that anyone could heal as he did . . . and possibly even MORE!

Healing was considered as much a part of the early Christian ministry as preaching and the sacraments. The Bible tells us that the apostles followed Jesus' lead and describes them curing all manner of maladies such as dysentery, blindness, leprosy, and snakebite. Unfortunately these achievements led to the belief that only Christians could heal, through Jesus. Even so, the religious use of healing declined slowly over the next few hundred years but was carried on by many of the kings of Europe. Known as the "royal touch" it seems that the power to heal was such a revered "gift" that it could hold the entire populace in awe and thus commanded immense respect from the king's subjects. Although royal healing can be traced back to King Pyrrhus of Epirus in the third century BC, it wasn't until the eleventh century with the reign of Edward the Confessor, that it became extremely popular—a popularity that lasted for seven centuries until the reign of sceptical William IV. During the reign of Charles II, it is recorded that he touched 90,798 sufferers in nineteen years. The sick even had raw sores touched by the monarchs and were then blessed.

Many of these earlier recorded healings were accredited to the power of Jesus, a divine power inborn in a monarch, or a divine gift inherent in the healer but there were also contemporary medical theorists who felt that the forces and influences of nature were the source of these healing effects.

In the 16th century Paracelsus, in addition to his discoveries in drug therapies, founded the theory of a sympathetic system of medicine in which he said there was a link between humans and the heavens above. This link was seen as *"a pervasive magnetic fluid, which existed throughout the universe, pervaded all space and possessed unique qualities of healing."* He also said, that if this force was wielded by someone, then that person could heal disease in others. *"The vital force,"* he said, *"was not enclosed inside an individual but radiated within and around him or her like a luminous sphere, which could be made to act at a distance."* There is no doubt he was refering to the human aura and the effect of distance (absent) healing!

In 1778, a radical French healer stated that he could achieve remarkable therapeutic success without the need for the patient's faith in himself or Christ. Franz Mesmer claimed that the healing results he achieved came through the use of a universal energy that he called 'fluidum', which he described as; *"a subtle physical fluid that fills the universe and is the connecting medium between people, all living things, the earth and other heavenly bodies."* Mezmer theorized that if disharmony occurred between the physical body and these subtle forces of nature, sickness was the end result. He realised that the life sustaining and regulating actions of the fluidum were integral to the basic processes of homeostasis and health.

Mesmer came to realise that the best source of this universal healing force was the human body itself. He felt that *the most active points of energy flow were from the palms of the hands*. By placing the practitioner's hands on patients for direct healing, energy was allowed a direct route to flow from healer to patient.

More recent laboratory investigations into the physiological effects of laying-on-of-hands has confirmed the magnetic nature of these subtle healing energies particularly in relation to his theory that magnets passed over a body acted as a conductor creating an energy pathway for the healing energies to follow. Researchers have demonstrated that Mesmer's understanding of the magnetic nature of the subtle energies of the human body was centuries ahead of his contemporaries.

Mesmer also discovered that water could be charged by this mysterious healing energy and that the power stored in bottles of energised water could be transmitted to a patient by way of metallic rods held in the their hands. Drinking the water later proved to be just as effective—interestingly, one of the qualities of Orgone is that it is readily absorbed by water. Later scientists would prove that the healing energies could also be transmitted via other mediums, such as clothing or cloth.

Anecdote

In the autumn of 1995 I had a vivid dream in which I was directed to take my wife Caterina, a gifted healer, to the Philippines to receive instruction on opening the body to effect healing. On arrival we were directed to a young Philippino psychic surgeon who claimed he knew in advance that we were coming.

During those two weeks, in a tin shed at the rear of his modest home, he willing gave her instruction and guidance to enable her to enter the body with her hands. In nightly conversations with

Ambrosio we learned that he was handed the gift of healing from his mother who, in turn, received it from her mother. He could trace the ability to heal in his family back five generations to a time when there was no allopathic alternative available in the remote mountainous regions.

His ancestors were indigenous tribes isolated in the dense jungle forests in the mountains of Northern Luzon. All family and tribal healing was done by the tribal healer with natural herbs and divine energies, including surgical operations if necessary. The operations were carried out without anaesthesia or asepsis and yet were painless and had little or no side effects. The ability to heal in this manner was passed to a select person in each generation. Philippino psychic healers still heal in this manner to this day.

Summary

- Energy Healing has been documented as long ago as 3500 years.

- Shamans, healer-priests and medicine men have been known to produce healing effects throughout recorded history.

- Hippocrates, the father of modern medicine was an energy healer.

- Christ healed and said; *"These things that I do so can ye do, and more."*

- Franz Mezmer discovered that water could be energized and then consumed for a healing effect.

- Mezmer maintained that the most powerful points for the transfer of healing energies are the palm of the hands.

CHAPTER TWO

SCIENTIFIC EVIDENCE

"Healers do indeed possess some type of bio-energetic influence that affects the cellular expression of disease states" [4]

In the 1960s reputed scientist, Dr Bernard Grad, of McGill University, Canada, carried out extensive tests, under stringent control conditions, of the measurable effects of energy healing. Grad scientifically verified the therapeutic power of spiritual healers and psychic healers. In his laboratory tests with mice he was able to prove that healers could:

- significantly retard the growth of tumours,

- prevent the development of tumours,

- transfer their healing energies via an organic storage

medium, such as cotton wool or fabric, to patients
with the same successful results, and

• speed the healing of wounds.

In one experiment he removed small patches of skin from
forty-eight mice then divided them into three groups. One group
was left untouched. The second was treated by healer Oskar
Estebany, who laid his hand upon their backs, and the third group
were exposed to a heat similar to that of the healer's hands. The
wounds of the mice treated by Estebany healed much quicker
than the other two groups. Dr Grad repeated this experiment
using 300 mice with exactly the same results.

Grad then went on to test the effects of human energy healing
on plants using the medium of water. His experiments, using
barley seeds exposed to healer-treated saline water (a known
retardant of plant growth), proved that the healer-treated water
produced a higher strike rate, were more abundant in yield, larger
in plant size and contained more chlorophyll than the growth
from seeds exposed to untreated saline water.

In another remarkable experiment he compared plants that
had been fed healer energized water with those fed water energized
by mental patients suffering from severe depression. The plants
energised by the healer demonstrated a higher than normal growth
rate, whereas water treated by the severely depressed patient
produced a retarded rate and distorted plant growth!

This and other experiments carried out by Dr Grad
determined that healing energies possess both negative and positive
polarity. His experiments concluded that *"healers appear to possess
energy of a strong positive, nurturing nature, while severely depressed
or negative individuals give off negative energy that inhibits growth."*

In Grad's laboratory experiments with healer-energized water
he was able to prove what Mezmer theorized two centuries before,
that water underwent a significant change in cellular structure
through a disruption to its hydrogen bonding and a shift in the

atomic bond angle of its molecules. In addition, the healer energy not only 'charged' the water but also decreased its surface tension. This experiment scientifically verified that healer-energized water could have a therapeutic effect when ingested by a patient.

Another researcher doing similar work was the Rev. Franklin Loehr, a congregational minister with a degree in chemistry. Loehr used 150 volunteers trained in disciplined prayer to concentrate on 27,000 seeds. More than 100,000 measurements were taken that revealed a superior result with the growth of plants receiving prayer to those that did not.

In the mid 1970s an American research chemist, Dr Robert Miller, noted a similarity between magnetised water and healer-energized water. The question raised by this observation was; is the healing energy of a healer simply a magnetic force? Miller was unable to prove that a difference existed, despite extensive scientific tests. It was left to an enzymologist, Dr Justa Smith, in her experiments with the effects of healing on enzymes, to provide the evidence that, whilst healer energy appeared to be magnetic in nature, it has an amazing **selective metabolic reasoning** that magnetic energy does not have. Magnetism causes the cells to grow whether it is beneficial to the organism or not. Dr Smith proved that healer-energy seems to possess a kind of **innate intelligence** that can cause variable changes within cells, but *"always in a direction of greater benefit of the cells, and thus the organism."* This offered an explanation as to why undesirable cells such as those contained within tumours or disease would die off or decline when treated by healers.

Following this discovery, a team of scientists in Oregon planned a series of experiments in which they endeavoured to show that an application of energy from the hands of a healer would boost a patient's total energetic system back into homeostasis (metabolic equilibrium). The experiments succeeded in proving that the *"healer's energetic boost has special, self-organizational properties that assist the cells in creating order from disorder along defined routes of cellular expression."* In other words, a healer's energy enhances an organism's own ability to increase order thereby assisting the body to heal itself—a kind of physiological reboot.

Experiments involving the young English healer Matthew Manning proved the measurable effects of healing on human cells. One of the tests involved human blood cells in which Manning undertook to control the release of haemoglobin from stressed red blood cells by slowing down their release into a saline solution. He was asked to concentrate on the cells to prevent them from being broken down.

> *"There was a sequence of five trials during which I was to exert a healing influence, and five trials during which for control purposes I removed my influence. During one of the trials I was placed in a distant room and had to influence the cells from 30 metres away. The scientists then accurately measured the extent to which the cells broke down by placing the tubes in a machine called a spectrophotometer, which measured the amount of light being transmitted through the solution. This time the results, when measured statistically, beat chance by over 100,000 to one. Most interestingly, it was found that the one trial where I influenced the blood cells from 30 metres away produced the greatest response!*
>
> *In his report, Dr Braud wrote: 'The major conclusion to be drawn from these experiments is that Matthew Manning was able to exert significant psychokinetic influences upon a variety of biological targets."* [5]

Another healer, Dean Kraft, was invited to participate in a series of carefully controlled experiments at the Science Unlimited Research Foundation in San Antonio to see if his healing influence could kill cancer cells. A particularly virulent strand of cancer cells was placed into a number of flasks. The healer was told to concentrate on one flask to kill the cells, another flask was held by a young man who was told to copy everything the healer did and the third was left unattended. The kill rate of cancer cells in the healer held flask was 300 percent higher than either of the other two flasks. The flask held by the young man was no different to the unattended flask.

Later, this series of tests was again conducted with Matthew Manning as the healer.

> *"The results were the most dramatic that I had achieved in any experiments. It was observed that there was a marked increase in the number of detached, and therefore dead, cancer cells in the flasks on which I had been concentrating, yet there was no changes in any of the flasks treated by the volunteer. The number of dead cells had increased in those trails by between 200 percent and 1200 percent. One of the interesting features of this experiment was that I was able to exert a very significant influence over the cells even when I was contained within a shielded room. This suggests that whatever was causing the healing was not electricity, magnetism or electromagnetism as none of those forces could have penetrated outside the shielded room."*[6]

A fascinating aspect of these experiments is the fact the healers were able to effect an improvement or a demise of the cells. Asked to kill cancer cells they did so. Asked to make blood cells last longer, they did so. Does this mean that the healing power has the intelligence to identify those organisms or cells that need a boost and those that must be eradicated?

During the past 500 years many scientists have conducted extensive, carefully controlled, experiments to prove that healing energies exist, and that humans have the ability to convey healing energies to one another to bring about therapeutic effects within their metabolism by direct touch or at a distance. The great scientist Nicola Tesla was quoted as saying; *"In that single decade when science first begins to investigate the non physical, they will make more progress in that decade than they have made in the past century."*

Anecdote

In our work with the Brazilian Spiritual Healer, Joao Teixeira da Faria, we have had numerous opportunities to observe the scepticism of many western-trained doctors who, following observation and stringent examination of his work, depart with their scepticism crushed and their beliefs questioned. One such team was from the Brazilian Faculty of Medicine, Federal University de Juis de Fora. Minas Gerias, Brazil.

The following is the results of their investigation as reported in the popular magazine O IDEAL;

> *"Notwithstanding the fact that Spiritual Surgery has been lacking in serious research from a scientific viewpoint, it has greatly interested the media and the public in general. It is clearly noticeable that most of the opinions expressed on the subject in newspapers, television and magazines are expressed from a preconceived point of view, either favourable or unfavourable according to the individual's conviction.*
>
> *According to Marlene Nobre, president of the Brazilian Spiritistic-Medical Association, many medium healers are looked upon with reservation due to the lack of deeper studies on the subject. We decided to conduct a careful study.*
>
> *Notwithstanding the fact that thousands of people in the world are healed in this unorthodox way, many researchers refuse to study the matter, assuming that it is nothing but fraud. That the cuts are tricks, the blood only dye and the fragments extracted from patients*

are of animal origin. Unfortunately this opinion is reinforced by those spiritual surgeons, the world over, who refuse to allow the removal of tissue for scientific examination.

In our study we sought the assistance of the Pathology Department of the University Hospital. Our aim was to establish whether these phenomena are frauds or of a positive nature requiring further studies. We chose, as our subject, the medium from Goiana, Joao Teixeira de Faria, who works in the town of Abadiania, because he treats over 1000 people per day and is constantly in the media for treating internationally famous people.

The medium Joao has only an elementary schooling, he is the owner of a ranch in Anapolis and he provides treatment (free of charge) in a centre which does not bear a spirititist title. He has a strong and decisive personality but each of the spirits he incorporates manifest their own personality, some kind, some rude and some firm.

It was observed that groups arrived every Wednesday, Thursday and Friday from every part of Brazil. They received treatment for various ailments by one or more spirit entities, manifesting themselves in Joao Teixeira, either by natural herbs or by spiritual surgery if required.

According to a statement by the centre, there is no need for visible surgery (with incisions) as all treatment can be done by invisible surgery (an operation effected through the spiritual body). The choice is the patient's. We decided to study the visible surgery, carried out before the waiting crowds. We filmed and photographed a series of operations, the patients were interviewed and examined and all of the organic substances were collected and removed for pathological testing at the university.

None of the patients received any form of anaesthetic and only one of them said they felt a mild form of pain during the operation. The instruments used were mostly kitchen knives or bistoury (surgical knife). No form of antiseptic was observed.

We observed a series of operations including; scraping the eye cornea, the introduction of scissors-shaped tweezers tipped with cotton wool into the nasal cavity, the extraction of teeth, breast surgery and abdominal surgery and the surgical removal of a lymphoma (benign tumour) weighing 120 grams from a patient's back.

Our conclusions firmly uphold that the surgery is genuine. The pathological tests reveal that the removed substances are compatible with their origins and that they are human tissues.

We contend that further studies are urgently needed to deepen our knowledge of this subject. In particular the following should be investigated; the lack of pain during physical surgery even without anaesthesia, and the absence of asepsis. It is our recommendation that science should urgently devote more serious research into this matter that could effect the life of millions throughout the world."

We concur.

Summary

- A universal healing energy exists.

- The human body is the best channel of healing energy.

- The most active points of human energy flow are from the palms of the hands.

- Healing energy is magnetic in nature but intelligently selective toward a beneficial result to the patient.

- Human applied energies can retard the growth and development of tumours.

- Healer energies will speed the healing of wounds.

- Healing energies can be transferred by an organic storage medium like cotton.

- Water can store healing energies and transfer it to others for therapeutic effect.

- Water is structurally changed when energized by healers.

- Healer energies promote plant growth.

- Human healing energies seem to have innate intelligence, which always creates a change within the molecular structure of cells towards the greater benefit of the organism.

- Healing energies will boost a patient's energy system back into homeostasis.

- Healing energies can be applied by contact or at a distance.

- Healers possess energies of a strong, nurturing nature. Depressed or negative individuals produce negative, inhibiting energy.

CHAPTER THREE

TYPES OF ENERGY HEALING

Healing by any name is healing still.

Today, healing courses are available under a myriad of commercial names; Reiki (Usui, Tera-mai, Ascension, Tibetan, Jin Kei Do), Sekhem, Prana, Qi-Gong, Mahikari, Hankuna, Karuna, Spiritual Healing, Psychic Healing, Magnetic Healing, Cranial Sacral Therapy and many others. All of these can be assumed to be "energy healing".

Some definitions:

> PRANA: It is difficult to define Prana Therapy because it varies between countries and schools of teaching. In Australia it is taught as treating only the energy fields—there is no physical contact with the body. In the Philippines it treats both the energy fields and the body in direct application

of energy, whilst in Europe it is physically applied with hand-to-body contact similar to Reiki.

REIKI: Reiki is manually applied energy direct to the body. It is a direct transfer of universal energy from and through the therapist to the patient. There are many varieties of Reiki, each adjusted to suit the particular beliefs and view points of the course teachers and promoters.

QI-GONG: is an ancient Chinese art of harnessing Chi (or Qi) energy, which, with concentration and practice, can be used for self-defence as well as for healing and diagnostics.

MAGNETIC energy is that generated by our own bio-energy bodies or introduced from an external source. As it is transferred from the therapist to the patient, the therapist becomes depleted and needs to be replenished from the universal source.

PSYCHIC SURGERY is performed by drawing on universal energies delivered by the Holy Spirit for the specific purpose of surgery. Intense prayer is offered in which the medium calls on the Divine to supply the energy for the operation/ treatment. During surgery the medium concentrates energy from his/her hands pointed at a particular location on the body until the fingers or the hand break through into the body of the patient. As if an invisible laser beam were emanating from the fingers, the flesh opens during trance concentration with only moderate pressure upon the skin. The incision is closed with just a wipe of the hand. There is only a little post-operative bleeding and no anaesthetic or asepsis is required. This type of therapy is normally focused on a specific task—the removal of a tumour or cyst—although these healing mediums also practice non-invasive magnetic healing.

In SPIRITUAL HEALING the therapist is an attuned vessel for the transmission of the healing energies as required for each individual patient. The healing energies are supplied by spirit guides, who use the therapists' body to deliver them to the patient to effect healing or surgery. Spiritual Healing treats all ailments— what is needed at the time is provided by the guides. It does not drain the therapist because he/she is simply a vessel through which the energy is transmitted. In fact it can be quite rejuvenating.

In addition there are a myriad of new, rediscovered or revamped therapies that utilize an energy input method. Cranial-Sacral Therapy, Myofascial Release, and other tactile therapies had their beginnings in the hands-on manipulation techniques of bones, muscles or connective tissues. In recent years breakaway groups focused more on the energy field and the fluctuating spirit that animates life, seeking the rhythmic pulsations of the body in which the body structures are seen as aspects of consciousness and spirit.

So what is the difference between these modalities? Very little it would seem.

There are of course differences in terminology, ideology, methods, rituals and application but if one looks for common threads there are many:

- All use the human body and mind of the therapist as the vessel to receive and deliver energy to the patient.

- The energy is directed to the client with good intent of the mind and heart.

- Most deliver the energy via their hands, either applied directly to the body or directed at the body from a distance.

- Some transfer the therapist's own magnetic energy—
  this can be depleting to the healer.

- Some connect to a "divine energy source" according to
  their preferred spiritual beliefs.

- Some call on assistance from spiritual entities to heal,
  energize and operate.

In this *Part 1*, we deal with the first four of the above similarities. The last two are covered in *Part 2—Spiritual Healing*.

All healing methods are effective in their own way and, notwithstanding the proclaimed advantages of one over another, they all have one common purpose: to heal, harmonize and energize. Despite their differences there are vital *common elements* in all of them. Without these key elements there is usually little result.

The Common Elements

The common elements are:

- LOVE. A love of our fellow human.

- COMPASSION. A genuine compassion for the
  recipient,

- DESIRE. A mind-directed desire to ease the suffering
  of our clients, and

- INTENT. Our intent to render help to our fellow
  human being.

The mind directed desire to ease the suffering of our fellow man with compassion, love and a positive intent is the key to all energy healing.

Most healing modalities have their own recommendations and regulations placed upon them by their governing bodies, schools or government regulations for the following reasons:

- Because it works for them

- It carries historic significance

- For control

- For profit, or

- Unfounded fear.

Simply put, all energy healings draw curative energies from the One Source. The method of attunement and application differs according to the ideals of the teachings and the restrictions they or society places upon the practitioner.

Providing the INTENT is clean, there are no taboos in energy healing. It is simple, logical, unrestricted, effective and safe.

The Difference Between Energy Healing and Spiritual Healing

Depending on the vibrational frequency from which a particular healer operates, we can see that there are a variety of energy levels at which healing can occur. On the one hand we have a phenomenon, which might be referred to as *energy healing*. This type of healing appears to require direct contact of the hands between the patient and the healer, or an intermediary of some energy storage medium such as water or cotton. Alternatively there is a different therapeutic method, which has been referred to as *spiritual healing*. The practitioners of this art usually attune themselves through meditation to the 'forces of the Divine' and, through attunement with spirit guides, mentally project energy to the sick individual by the direct laying-on-of-hands or at a distance.

It is most likely that *energy healing* takes place mainly at the level of the physical body and at the first etheric energy layer. There is a direct transfer of energy from the healer to the patient, mostly through the intermediary of the hands. There are actually minor charkas in the palms of the hands that act as centres of energy flow into and out of the body. However, *spiritual healing* **is able to interact with, not only the physical body and first etheric layer but with the higher levels as well.**

In contradistinction to *energy healing*, *spiritual healing* works at the level of the higher subtle energies and chakras to effect a healing from the most primary level of disease origins. The spiritual healer works as a power source of multiple frequency outputs to allow energy shifts at several levels simultaneously. While most energy healers work only at the level of the body, **spiritual healers usually work with the many levels of the mind and spirit as well.** The nature of this higher dimensional energy is that it transcends all limitations of space and time by virtue of the fact that levels from the etheric and higher energies are in the domain of negative space/time. As such, the energies working at these levels move in a dimension that is outside of the usual reference of ordinary (positive) space/time in which the conscious mind has limited perception. The frequencies at which spiritual healing takes place often extend to the same levels at which the Higher Self exists and operates.

Spiritual healers operate primarily at, what scientists call, the *negative space/time levels* **of people's higher dimensional components that feed, organize and support the molecular/ cellular structures of the physical body.**[7]

It is necessary to recognize that there is NO ALL-CURING PANACEA FOR ALL HUMAN ILLS. There is no single treatment, pill, tonic, therapy or herb that will cure all. Whilst many diseases do respond to a single treatment type, some require a combination of treatments to effect a satisfactory cure. Undoubtedly, energy therapies alone can prompt a cellular life force stimulation, which often produces seemingly "miraculous" results. Even so, all good therapists will recognize that complementary input from herbs, vitamins, medicine, massage, skeletal manipulation, colonic irrigation or dietary change as being highly complimentary and often imperative.

Some knowledge of interrelated medical strands such as allopathic, homeopathic, naturopathic, herbal, colonic irrigation, chiropractic, osteopathic, therapeutic massage etc. enables the healer to understand how they fit together and compliment each other to achieve a holistic result. It is important to be able to communicate with other health professionals effectively and, when necessary, refer patients for supplementary treatment.

Most energy therapies normally require a number of treatments. Each session prepares the body for deeper treatment or spiritual surgery, but sessions are normally spaced a few days apart to allow the body time to effect cellular change.

Anecdote

In Austrlaia in mid 1995 I signed up for a course in Pranic Healing. I wanted to know if it differed widely from other forms of energy therapies. It did. Not only did it differ from other modalities, it varied from other Pranic teachings across the world. The practice of this particular school strictly limited the contact of healer and patient. The energy was to be delivered at a distance of two to three meters, without hand or body contact.

Some months later we were in the Philippines where the use of Pranic healing is widespread. Here the method was quite different—it required the use of a laying-on-of-hands style and very little healing from a distance. We began to suspect that the conductors of these courses make up their own rules to suit themselves. Later, in Italy, we were to observe practices that supported our suspicions.

Pranic Healing was ridiculed by the Italian media prompted by the medical profession who saw it as a threat to their income. Fortunately the Florence School of Pranic Healing was headed by a retired medical doctor who pursued legal recognition fervently. Eventually the medical profession caved in and embraced the therapy with enthusiasm, seeing it as a way to make easy money for themselves. The result was a sham. Some unscrupulous doctors offered ten minutes of medically sanctioned Prana Therapy that amounted to nothing less than laying the patient in a prone position, touching them on the forehead and setting a timer to ten minutes. The doctor then left the room until the time expired. For this he charged an exorbitant fee. Little wonder it has taken more than ten years for Italian Prana Therapists to regain the public trust they lost in this farce to make money.

We had the privilege to lecture at the Italian School of Prana Therapy where they follow a similar technique to that used in most forms of Reiki.

Summary

- The term *Energy Healing* can be used to cover all modalities.

- The common elements are LOVE, COMPASSION, MIND DIRECTED DESIRE to ease suffering, and INTENT.

- *Spiritual Healing* differs from all other modalities by the calling of spiritual entities to use the therapist as a conductor of healing energies.

- *Spiritual Healing* is able to operate primarily at the *negative space/time levels* of people's higher dimensional components that feed, organize and support the molecular/cellular structures of the physical body.

In all forms of modern energy healing it is necessary to:

- maintain an open attitude

- recognize the part the healer plays in the whole medical picture

- have adequate understanding of:

  - counselling methods
  - anatomy
  - massage technique

  as well as some appreciation of:

  - allopathic medicine
  - homeopathy
  - acupuncture
  - naturopathy
  - nutrition herbal medicine, and
  - osteopathy.

CHAPTER FOUR

ENERGIES

The ability of humans to tap into and deliver unseen
energies is the fundamental basis of all energy healing.

Recognized Energies

There is a vast range of known energy forms used by us all in everyday life. It is worth reflecting on the shortness of time since we discovered and accepted common energies used today; electricity received wide acceptance less than one hundred years ago, radar less than seventy years, microwaves only twenty-five years, lasers a mere twenty. Each new discovery is at first ridiculed and then embraced as "conventional". Today we still see much ignorance in the field of Bio-energies—the energies of the human body.

The Energy Frequency Spectrum Chart (Fig. 1) lists all known energy frequencies. The narrow band attributable to colour and visible light is but a small fraction of the whole band and yet the average person believes only in what they can see. According to research scientist Dr John Ott[8], *"the human eye sees less than 1 percent of the total electromagnetic spectrum. Little is known about the mysterious light sources at either end of the visible spectrum— the ultraviolet, infrared and background radiation—but evidence now seems to indicate that they exert a profound influence on the physical and mental health of animals, plants and man."*

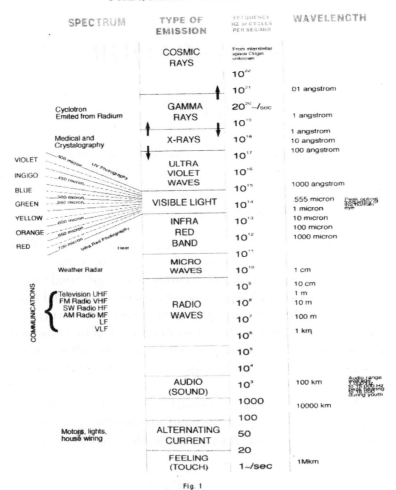

Fig. 1

Almost all of the bands between Gamma Rays and Alternating Current have only been accepted and put to practical use within the past 100 years and yet, within these frequencies exist many sub frequencies that remain as yet undiscovered by established science. As recently as year 2000, Dr Ron Hruby discovered a previously unknown form of magnetism in experiments in meditation/visualization conducted on a subject ten miles distant. Why is it so hard to accept then, that as an energy entity, the human body can absorb, transmit and filter energies from the complex energy atmosphere within which it evolved?

The universe is made up of an incomprehensible collection of invisible life force energies—a vast ocean of energies. Just as we live in a solid or material world, we also live in a non-material, non-solid, invisible world. The air we breathe and the rays of the sun are invisible and yet they are vital to the creation and continuation of life itself. In every part of the cosmos, this ocean of invisible life force is in a constant state of motion and interaction. Every molecule, every substance, form or component of the universe has its own energy field, vibrational frequency, motion pattern and level of interaction according to its own unique capacity. And yet, no one thing is separated from the next—all are interconnected.

WE ARE ENERGY BEINGS!

Einstein's accepted theory of relativity states that "*matter and energy are interchangeable (E=mc²).*" Mass is nothing but condensed, slowed down or crystallized energy. OUR BODIES ARE SIMPLY CONDENSED ENERGY.

In addition to the electromagnetic impulses that course the cells of our condensed physical body, we have two other life-force energies;

- The *Ethereal (Energy) Body*, which includes the chi meridians, the seven auric layers and their corresponding chakras and the vital life force carried throughout our lifetime. Your energy body is the counterpart of your physical body and it is more responsive that your physical body to many influences. Because it holds the blueprint of the state of your physical body, it is the focal point of healing.

- The *Life Force of the Soul*, which consists of the mind, consciousness, memory and personality guided by the indwelling fragment of God. The soul is the sum total of your aggregate self—who you really are—your eternal personality that, according to reincarnationalists, carries with it the plan of what you have come to do in this lifetime, based on what you achieved or failed to achieve in past lives. It is the sum total of your experiential existence.

Ultimately our total life force energy is affected by the subtle energy of our own thoughts and how these thoughts influence our destiny and shape the personality of the soul as it strives to elevate to perfection.

THE HUMAN BODY IS A KALEIDOSCOPE OF ENERGY INTERACTION

"Seen from the inside, the human creature demonstrates an amazing kaleidoscopic—a mutable phenomenon. Bodies, or rather aggregates of atomic units, fade out and disappear, or flash again into manifestation. Streams of colours pass and repass; they twine or intertwine. Certain areas will then suddenly intensify their brightness and blaze forth with brilliance; or again they can be seen dying out and certain areas will be colourless and apparently non-existent. But always there is a persistent over-shadowing light, from which a stream of light pours

*down into the phenomenal man; this can be seen
attaching itself in two major localities of the dense inner
core of physical man. These two points of attachment
are to be found in the head and the heart. There can
also be seen seven other paler disks of light which are
evidence of the seven centres (chakras)."*

This view into the kaleidoscope of intertwining energies
within the human body provides a colourful and spectacular image
of the continual flow, birth, death, subtleties and beauty of life-
force energies within us.

HUMANS GENERATE, RECEIVE, CONDUCT AND TRANSMIT ENERGY

Energies from the Sun, the Earth and the Universe penetrate
every cell in your physical body and vitalize your energy body.
Your energy body is continually interacting with the energies
around it in a perpetual cycle of repair and rejuvenation. They
penetrate, absorb, transform, harmonize, are spent and expended
in a constant stream. They are our energy quintessence.

We exist because we are a conscious life force and the
sustenance of our life force is energy. All day, every day, we utilise
energy to achieve even the smallest task. When we think, we
concentrate energy to the mind—thought is energy—at the same
time reducing the amount of energy available for other tasks.
SEXUAL intercourse is a concentration of energy into the lower
chakra area. BODY ELIMINATIONS concentrate energy into
the intestine and bladder. BIRTH requires an enormous amount
of energy into the pelvic region. Any great athlete will concede
that to achieve excellence in sport, one must concentrate all energy
and mind focus to the given task.

**As healers we must learn to utilise and direct healing
energies to bring about a molecular change within the body
of the recipient.**

We live in a dense ocean of energies. Just within the electromagnetic spectrum there are many forms: microwave, radar, short wave, medium wave and long wave radio, television, electricity, and magnetism. There is little doubt that excessive and long term exposure to these powerful electromagnetic fields can seriously affect human biology—a compelling public health issue—however there are many electromagnetic energies that are beneficial to human biological systems. Their effects in the treatment of serious diseases, as researched and published by respected American scientists, Robert Becker and Paul Brodeur, prove the point. Becker and Brodeur refer to advances in the fields of electro-therapy, transcutaneous electrical nerve stimulation, electro-acupuncture, pulse magnetic fields and nuclear magnetic resonance imaging, all of which produce some positive effects for humanity by working with the body's subtle electric and magnetic fields.

Unrecognised Energies

Canadian scientist, John Hutchison stunned the scientific world when he harnessed hitherto unknown energies. With basic electronic equipment, he created phenomena within the structure of solid materials that resulted in levitation of heavy objects, disintegration of steel bars, brass rods that exploded from the inside out and the total disappearance of large objects. Hutchison called this energy *Zero Point Jitter* explaining the phenomena as "*a combination of known energies, psychic focus and accessing a doorway between the physical and the spiritual dimensions.*"[10] It is known today as the *'Hutchison Effect'*. Hutchison also discovered that limitless energy was available by harnessing the energy inherent in crystalline rocks. He proved that all solid matter had the ability to extract energy from the Earth Grid in perpetual replenishment, hence, crystalline rocks could supply endless energy for human consumption. Hardly surprisingly Hutchison came under intense pressure and threats to his life not long after he demonstrated that small batteries supplying endless energy could be made from simple crystalline rocks, a process that would eliminate the harmful environmental effects of dry cell battery manufacture.

So Where Does the Energy Come From?

Throughout all organized space there are gravity responding energy currents, power circuits, ultimatonic activities and organizing electronic energies. In our local universe there are 100 octaves (groups) of energy manifestations. The visible spectrum on earth is only a single octave range. Only sixty-four octaves are recognized on earth, the remaining thirty six are still undiscovered.[11] Our planet is covered with an intricate network of energy known as the *Earth Grid*. This grid acts like a unified tuning fork vibrating with our Light/Life/Electromagnetic Spectrum. It is fed constantly from the astrophysical centre of our local solar system—the Sun. Our molecular bodies and human consciousness, as we walk on the Earth, live within this grid. It is the pervasive means for the harmonious fusion of the energies of the solar system into human consciousness.

The Grid is the forgotten nexus between mankind as embodied living consciousness and the entire universal existence. It is the spiritual and energy link for the blending of cosmic and terrestrial energies of the human reality.[12]

The connecting thread of this bewildering grid of spiritual and physical life on Earth is the *Ley Line*. Ley lines are the subtle luminous strands that lead to the planetary grid, the primary light and energy matrix, creating, enveloping and maintaining our planet Earth. Described as *"a geometrically precise web, punctuated with grids of light focal points. A receptor web complex covering the globe with pulses or lines, which make a coloured spinning membrane. A great web of patterning oscillations and quavering of energy".*[13] This great energy ocean is often referred to as the Universal Energy Field (UEF).

The Universal Energy Field (UEF)

According to physicist Barbara Brennan: *"The UEF is composed of an energy previously undefined by western science. The UEF may exist between matter and energy. Some scientists refer to the phenomenon of UEF as bio-plasma."*[14]

She quotes scientists Dr John White and Dr Stanley Krippner as stating; *"the UEF permeates all space, animate and inanimate objects, and connects all objects to each other. It flows from one object to another and its density varies inversely with the distance from its source."*[15]

She adds, *"Visual observations reveal the field to be highly organized in a series of geometric points, isolated pulsating points of light, spirals, webs of lines, sparks and clouds. It is always associated with some form of consciousness, from highly developed to very primitive. Highly developed consciousness is associated with higher vibrations and energy fields."*[16]

The UEF is the source of energy absorbed through the seven primary energy centres (chakras) of the human etheric body. Healing energy from the UEF can be directed by a correctly attuned healer to a patient. The UEF is also the information storage hologram, the energetic imprint of everything that has happened or has ever been known—hence it is **the medium by which a correctly attuned person (medium) can access past/ future time dimensions and knowledge and perform distant diagnostics.**

Effects of Healing Energies on the Human Body

In 1960 scientist Robert Becker made a profound discovery. He called it 'dedifferentiation'. *"What we found was astonishing,"* said Becker in the course of studying the energy current of injury in frogs. Becker discovered that the intended function of cells could be changed, or 'dedifferentiated', and directed towards healing and regeneration. The red blood cells could be dedifferentiated by applying exceedingly small amounts of electrical current (measured in billionths of amperes!). *"In less than an hour we could watch a red corpuscle change from a cell filled with haemoglobin and a small shrivelled nucleus, to a cell with no haemoglobin and a large active nucleus."*[17] The natural conclusion was that *minute applications of energy could control, reverse and even start human growth processes.*

Becker's discovery suggested that there was a medical revolution underfoot. *"The old chemical-mechanistic paradigm of medicine is crumbling away,"* he said, *"what is replacing it is a 'totally new paradigm' of life energy—'the hidden dynamic in medicine'. This new concept of life energy proposes a therapeutic effect on biological organisms from invisible magnetic, electric or electromagnetic energies—a host of new or rediscovered 'old' mediated healings are turning on the body's healing systems. Altogether, this trend is radically changing our conception of the human being and the nature and potential of healing."*

What Becker observed was a life reversal process within living cells due to applied energies, such as is delivered by healers. The energy, whilst minute, is powerful enough to stimulate human cells at a molecular level. When scientists examine a cell to its smallest observable quark they find nothing—no solid nucleus. Just a vortex of swirling energy! It is not surprising then that an application of external energy from a parallel biological energy source (human) would have a stimulating, invigorating and healing effect upon the cells of a receiving body.

Energy Effects on Cell Memory

According to American scientist Dr Hudson Hoagland, 500 million cells die in the human body every day. All protein, of which the human body is largely made up, is replaced every 180 days. This means that the body we see today is different to the one we had five months ago. Why is it then that the body stays the same and maladies remain? Long-term memory is stored in the DNA, which derives its blueprint from the master memory, stored in the ethereal body (the aura). This long-term master memory blueprint is the storehouse of thousands of years of evolutionary development and life experiences. Newer more recent memories of the body's latest status are stored within the cells. When cells reach the end of their cycle they pass on the most recent memories to the new cells including any improvements, imbalances or disease currently endured. Hence, if the body is unwell at the time of the transfer, the cell passes on the memory of the imbalance and the illness continues until the condition is reversed or the memory is changed.

When a healer intercedes by directing energy into the physical or ethereal bodies, guided by a thought-directed desire to bring about healing, the cell memory is changed. The cell looks to the DNA to retrieve the blueprint memory from the ethereal layers for guidance to return to the preferred balanced state of health.

Harry Edwards, the renown English healer who healed millions in his lifetime and who, at the time of his death in 1976, was receiving 8000 letters per week requesting absent healing, confirmed the effect of healing energy on cells:

> *"In contact healing, the healer is the attuned receiver through whom the energies are received for transmission to the patient. The energies produce chemical and physical reactions within the patient at a cellular level."* [18]

It would be hard to capsulate a more concise description of healing than that!

Can We See Energies?

Clairvoyance

Whilst many gifted mediums can "see" energies and bio-energy fields (auras) in varying degrees of clarity, the average person cannot. Being able to see the layers of the human aura improves, with time and application, as clairvoyant vision "opens." At first you may only see those layers closest to the body in faint blurred colours and forms. As you progress, you will sensitise yourself to higher frequencies and more easily perceive individual layers. Some people never see auras but do develop intuitive sensitivity to their form and state of vibrancy.

Diagnostic clairvoyants can clearly see distorted energy patterns in the aura of an unwell person. Others, whilst they cannot see the distortions, have developed the ability to perceive them sensitively.

Physical Observations

Most people can see orgone energy in the air quite easily. Orgone can be observed if you look for it against a blue sky—tiny white wriggling squiggles, which disappear almost as fast as you can focus on them. Orgone is a cosmic energy that all living matter absorbs continually. It is a part of the Universal Energy Field (UEF) from which we absorb and transmit healing energies. Orgone is an extraordinary energy source—it ranks as one of the most important energies applicable to life and healing. It has remarkable qualities that, carefully considered, offer a great many possibilities in the explanation of healing effects.

Dr Wilhelm Reich, one of the world's great scientists said: "*Orgone energy is the live cosmic energy of nature that fills the universe. It is a spontaneously pulsating, mass-free energy.*" Here are some of the accepted facts about orgone:

- It is mass free; that is, it has no inertia or weight.

- It negates the laws of entropy. Orgone energy flows from low concentrations to high concentrations—this is the process of creation.

- Matter is created from it.

- It is polarised—it can be either a positive or negative force.

- Penetrates or travels along all known materials except some plastics.

- It will pass through all materials, but at different speeds.

- Comes from our Sun in vast quantities.

- Is absorbed by water (our bodies are 90% water!).

- It is *affected by living beings,* that is, it is affected by our attitude and our thoughts!

- Orgone is absorbed by all natural matter on earth and is essential to the existence of all living things.

The energy aura from human hands may also be observed quite easily. Point the fingers of one hand towards the fingers of the other, observing them with unfocused vision. The energy will appear as a haze around the fingers that will attach itself to the energy of the opposite finger. It is sometimes seen in various colours, often as a light blue tint. The energy of the hands can be felt as well, like a tickling or spongy resistance; with palms facing together at a distance of around 10mm the energy can be felt as a resistance, as you move the palms in and out a little. There is a feeling of spongy pressure between them as the fields merge into one another.

Kirlian Photography

Thanks to the dedicated work of two Russians, Semyon and Valentina Kirlian, whose experiments with photographing the human energy field resulted in what is now known as Kirlian photography, the aura can now be caught on film. The method captures an image of the electro-magnetic energy emitted by any living matter, including human. It can be effectively used for diagnosis of disease, past or present, in the host body. What is extremely interesting and useful to healers is the visible proof it provides for three important facts:

- The human body is an energy body.

- The energy body reflects the condition of the physical body and visa versa.

- In a healing state, the host body represses its own energy and then utilises a finer more powerful energy channelled from the UEF.

Kirlian energy prints provide resounding proof that healers, during trance, set aside much of their own bio-energy and channel energy from an external source.

How Do Energies Enter the Human Body?

Life-force energies are introduced into the body in many forms; by food, light, colour, radiation, electro-magnetism, air, UEF and vibrations. These nourishing energies enter via a variety of pathways:

- Energies from the UEF are primarily induced through the Human Energy Field—the aura—and through their interconnecting chakras. Each chakra feeds and regulates the glands, nervous systems, blood vessels and organs within its zone of influence. The body can be divided into three major vertical zones (Fig 7):

Zone 1 Chakra 1 *Sexual*, testes, ovaries.
Chakra 2 *Abdominal*, intestines, womb, bladder.
Chakra 3 *Solar Plexus*, liver, kidneys, spleen, pancreas and adrenals.

Zone 2 Chakra 4 Heart, lungs, thymus.
Chakra 5 Throat, thyroid., parathyroid

Zone 3 Chakra 6 *Head*, pituitary, hypothalamus, endocrine gland, brain.
Chakra 7 *Crown*, spiritual, pineal gland.

- Energy is also extracted from food ingested through the stomach. This is a vital consideration as modern foods do not supply enough of the essential vitamins and minerals the body requires. Careful questioning during consultation should reveal these deficiencies.

- Orgone energy is absorbed directly through the skin and breathed into the lungs.

- Light and colour are absorbed by the skin and through the eyes. Light through the eyes feeds energy to the brain's cerebral cortex as well as the pituitary and pineal glands. Light energy directed by the pituitary affects the entire endocrine glandular system that controls the production and release of hormones. This regulates our body chemistry and its growth, all organs of the body, including our brain, and the autonomic nervous system throughout the body. Some light and colour is also directed via the retina through neurochemical channels to the pineal gland, situated behind the hypothalamus, to activate certain sensors in the brain connected with our sense of seasons, geographical location and our spiritual awareness.

* Electromagnetic energy and radiation absorbed via the skin and the HEF.

Energy is Directed by Thought

HEALING ENERGY may be directed by the DELIBERATE THOUGHT of the healer; via the HANDS and via the healer's ENERGY FIELD, to bring about a CHANGE WITHIN THE MOLECULAR STRUCTURE OF THE RECIPIENT'S BODY.

—THOUGHT is ENERGY.

—THOUGHT directs ENERGY.

—THOUGHT-DIRECTED ENERGY CREATES CHANGE within the MOLECULAR STRUCTURE of the HUMAN BODY.

Anecdote

I am one of the multitude who do not see auras. This is made all the more frustrating for me because I lived with a woman who does! If I am in deep thought she would often remark on the gentle hue of violet and blue emanating from my head. If I'm upset she would see red radiating in flashes and when I'm unwell she saw an antiseptic green aiding my body to heal. It has always been a mystery to me that, although I am constantly in the presence of powerful healers, I could not see their energy fields, until one day in Brazil.

I was watching the Brazilian healer Joao Teixeira in-entity

from the back of the crowd when unexpectedly I could see a golden helmet of light over the head of one of the house mediums. I was so fascinated by this sudden observation that I stared at it for some time. Then the thought occurred to me that, if this was the aura of a medium, Joao's must be really easy to see. To my surprise I could not see any aura around his head at all. I stared for some time and saw nothing as he performed an operation but, as he pulled away from the patient, the background moved as if I was observing it though a heat haze. His aura was so expanded that it was beyond my focused field of vision.

My ex-wife Caterina was gifted with auric vision and often she would remark about someone passing by; this one has a tumour in the stomach or that one has a drug problem. When I ask how she knows this she replies; "Because I see it in the aura." To her it was just a natural part of life, not imagining that others can´t see it too. This should not, however, deter those who cannot see energies. Many great healers exist that cannot see auras.

Summary

- Man understands only a small portion of the Universal Energy Field and utilizes less then 1% of the electromagnetic spectrum.

- All of space contains a vast range of energies still undiscovered—healers can conduct some of these energies to create healing change within the human body.

- We are energy beings. Our cells communicate via minute electrochemical impulses. Healer introduced energies can change that communication for the benefit of the patient.

- Our physical bodies are encased within a complex energy field called the Human Energy Field (HEF) or Aura.

- Humans receive, generate, conduct and transmit energies.

- Earth is covered by a matrix of energy Ley Lines, which are part of the Universal Energy Field (UEF).

- The UEF is the spiritual and energy link for the blending of cosmic and terrestrial energies of the human reality—it is our connection to all creation.

- The UEF is the primary source of energies absorbed by the human aura/chakra system.

- Healers can utilise and direct healing energies to initiate molecular change within the cells of a recipient's body and can alter the cell memory for the benefit of the organism.

- Some mediums can "see" energies.

- Orgone is one of the energies of the UEF and can be seen by most people. Orgone is the energy of creation. It permeates all known materials and is essential to the existence of all living things. Orgone is influenced by human thought.

- Energy is also derived from food, natural light and colour as well as from the UEF.

CHAPTER FIVE

CONCEPT OF DIVINE ENERGY

The God Concept.

The universe is not a place where nature's forces operate by chance. Every event that has happened from the beginning of time has happened according to certain laws inherent in our universe. These laws are the expressions of Universal Consciousness. Everything that exists, from the electron to the largest star, is impregnated with consciousness. This fundamental reality is so beyond our grasp that sages and saints have called it by a variety of terms. Many have termed it "God", some have called it "Law" and others "The Great Architect" or "All That Is". Each of us must determine how we will regard this divine consciousness that directs and connects everything. For convenience, let us call it GOD.[19]

There is a part inside each of us that is connected to each other—and we are all connected to everything, everywhere—some call it consciousness, others love. As a result of this connectedness, under the fundamental Laws that govern all creation, everything we do has an effect on the whole. A fine analogy of our connectedness to God is that of a massive mosaic depicting a picture of a resplendent king. Each small tile, seemingly insignificant by itself, represents a human soul. Each individual colour represents that soul's stage of enlightenment; a few fiery reds and oranges, calm blues and greens, some pure white, a few shining golds that adorn his crown, many dull uninteresting greys, and some black. Individually they are minuscule insignificant chips of fired clay but in the beauty of the whole each is dependent upon the other to create the majesty of the king. Even the loss of one tile can lessen the magnificence of the whole mosaic of All That Is.

The great medium and father of Spiritism, Allan Kardec, said; "*Spirits define God as the Supreme Intelligence, the Primary Reason of all Creation.*" They, spirits, refer to the immensity of worlds and dimensions that make up the cosmic universes. Such is the greatness, the magnitude, the order and harmony of all creation, infinitely beyond man's capability to comprehend, that it can only be attributed to the omnipotent creation of a supreme, all pervading intelligence.

"*God,*" Kardec wrote, "*cannot be perceived by men. Even after death, disposing of our material perceptive faculties, our spirit cannot fully perceive the divine nature of God.*

Man, even in his relatively inferior stage of evolution, has convincing proof of the existence of God by his reason and by his inner feelings. Rationally, it is not possible to conceive that there could be an effect without a cause. Realizing the immensity of the universe, the infinite expansion of space, the order and harmony of innumerable worlds. Seeing nature's abundance, including the miracle of the human species, the minerals with their admirable crystal forms, the infinite variety of flora, the animal kingdom with it's myriad variety of birds, beasts and insects and the microscopic world with its countless unicellular forms. All this vastness, profusion and beauty, oblige us to believe in God as a necessary creative cause. Even in the contemplation of our own physical body we see a miraculous work that can only be attributed to a divine creative force."

The old concepts of God have changed significantly over the past century. People everywhere question openly the religious model of a wrathful God who deals out punishment to sinners and wrongdoers. For some time in the post war era there was a void left in the minds of western society as to the reality of God. People lost faith in a God who "permitted" such inhuman atrocities. They blamed God instead of man, and the dogmas of religion no longer made sense in the minds of a better educated, free thinking society. Now, in the New Millennium, there is a new understanding of an all-permeating God as a Creative Force, a Universal Consciousness, a transcendent reality. All of which could well be true, for no one has ever succeeded in defining the God force, which is now accepted as existing in all creation as a binding, universal consciousness. If world religions cannot agree on an acceptable definition of God, what hope do we as individuals have?

Let's not dwell too long searching for a definitive description of God—scholars, through the ages, have failed to come to terms with it and have left us with a myriad of alternative names and descriptions. The best possible description comes from *The Urantia Papers*:

> "*God is primal reality in the spirit world; God is the source of truth in the mind spheres; God overshadows all throughout the material realms. To all created intelligences God is a personality, and to the universe of universes He is the First Source and Centre of eternal reality. God is neither manlike nor machinelike. The First Father is universal spirit, eternal truth, infinite reality, and father personality.*

The eternal God is infinitely more than reality realized or the universe personalized. God is not simply the supreme desire of man, the mortal quest objectified. Neither is God merely a concept, the power-potential of righteousness. The Universal Father is not a synonym for nature, neither is He natural law personified. God is a transcendent reality, not merely man's traditional concept of supreme values. God is not a psychological focalisation of spiritual meanings, neither is He the 'noblest work of man.' God may be any or all of these concepts in the minds of men, but He is more. He is a saving person and a loving Father to all who enjoy spiritual peace on earth, and who crave to experience personality survival after death.

The actuality of the existence of God is demonstrated in the human experience by the indwelling of the divine presence, the spirit Monitor sent from Paradise to live in the mortal mind of man and there to assist in evolving the immortal soul of eternal survival. The presence of this divine Adjuster in the human mind is disclosed by three experiential phenomena:

- *The intellectual capacity for knowing God—God-consciousness.*

- *The spiritual urge to find God—God-seeking, and*

- *The personality craving to be like God—the wholehearted desire to do the Father's will.*

The existence of God can never be proved by scientific experiment or by the pure reason of logical deduction. God can be realized only in the realms of human experience; nevertheless, the true concept of the reality of

*God is reasonable to logic, plausible to philosophy,
essential to religion, and indispensable to any hope of
personality survival.*

*Those who know God have experienced the fact of his
presence; such God knowing mortals hold in their
experience the only positive proof of the existence of the
living God which one human being can offer to another.
The existence of God is utterly beyond all possibility of
demonstration except for the contact between the God-
consciousness of the human mind and the God-presence
of the Thought Adjuster that indwells the mortal
intellect and is bestowed upon man as the free gift of the
Universal Father.*

*In theory you may think of God as the Creator, and he is
the personal creator of Paradise and the central universe
of perfection, but the universes of time and space are all
created and organized by the Paradise corps of the creator
Sons. The Universal Father is not the personal creator of
the local universe of Nebadon (in which Earth in
located); the universe in which you live is the creation of
his son Michael. Though the Father does not personally
create the evolutionary universes, he does control them in
many of their universal relationships and in certain of
their manifestations of physical, mindal, and spiritual
energies. God the Father is the personal creator of the
Paradise universe and, in association with the Eternal
Son, the creator of all other universe Creators.*

*As a physical controller in the material universe of
universes, the First Source and Centre functions in the
patterns of the eternal Isle of Paradise, and through this
absolute gravity centre the eternal God exercises cosmic
over-control of the physical level equally in the centre*

universe and throughout the universe of universes. As mind, God functions in the Deity of the Infinite Spirit; as spirit, God is manifest in the person of the Eternal Son and in the persons of the divine children of the Eternal Son. This interrelation of the First Source and Centre with the co-ordinate Persons and Absolutes of Paradise does not in the least preclude the direct personal action of the Universal Father throughout all creation and on all levels thereof. Through the presence of his fragmentised spirit the Creator Father maintains immediate contact with his creature children and his created universes.

God is spirit. He is universal spiritual presence. The Universal Father is an infinite spiritual reality; he is 'the sovereign, eternal, immortal, invisible, and only true God.' Even though you are the 'offspring of God,' you ought not to think that the Father is like yourselves in form and physique because you are said to be created 'in his image.' Spirit beings are real, notwithstanding they are invisible to human eyes; even though they have not flesh and blood."[20]

It is appropriate that we acknowledge what God is NOT:

- A man or woman,

- A wrathful punisher of all wrongdoers,

- An alien life-form as we envisage them,

- An all-knowing entity who records all pluses and minuses according to our behaviour, nor

- An impersonal force.

The use of the term "He" is, in a way, misleading because in many realities God is neither envisaged as human, male or female, for God is the origin of all sexes, all realities in some of which sex as we know it does not exist. In our earth records and in other realities God is known by many names: God Consciousness, Universal Father, Paradise Father, Divine Creator, First Source, Universe Centre, All That Is.

"When all is said and done, The Father idea is still the highest human concept of God" [21]

"God is perfect mind, which is love, wisdom and power. God is not a being but a force of good, which permeates the universe and is infinite. Evil is not a force, but an error in thought, which has arisen in the world because of the misuse of free will. It is finite and can be overcome by concentration on good and on God.

As God dwells within each of us, then every individual is part of the Whole that is God. Because we are all part of the Infinite Spirit of God, we cannot die. The gradual unfolding of the consciousness of the Mind of God within us is the process of evolution of our souls. In order to find God we must come to the realization that we are spiritual beings, and the acceptance of our personal responsibility for every action we commit. Thus the extent of our evolution depends entirely upon ourselves. As we desire, so shall we receive.

The universe is ordered by Divine law. If we go against it, the result is chaos. The first law is that of love. Love is the ability to see only latent perfection in our fellow men. Love is the attribute of the Divine mind, whereas fear stems from the material mind. Love and fear are the two incompatible opposites, the one forever striving to cast out the other. Love is the complete negation of self; self-interest is the father of fear. The natural expression of love is service to others, not so much in the performance of great works as in doing that which lies nearest to hand.

To dwell within the kingdom of heaven is to dwell within the Mind of God, which lies within ourselves. All must first seek this kingdom from which, once found, all else will flow. Prayer for ourselves is purposeless, for we already have all we ever need. The only true prayer is the unceasing communion with the divine spirit within us. Never must we forget that God is within us, not outside us, that we are all individual parts of God, which is the Whole.

God is there for all to see Him. You can see it in his creation. See the simple flower, its folding petals, its colour rare. In the heart of that small blossom, seek peace, God will be found. Stand on the hilltop and watch the setting sun, and in your heart be calm. Watch the blending of the colours as they fall behind the hills, and in that stillness, God will be. Stand among the yellow of the buttercups in the open fields when the dew lies upon the grass. Watch the bird rise with a flutter of wings, its throat trembling in the beauty of its note. It is there God will be found. In the laughter of a child when it runs to its mother's side; there too, will God be found. Find within your world the beauty of God and the wisdom of his kingdom, expressed in one word – Love."[22]

It is difficult to imagine any healer not having some concept of God. How that concept is perceived is a matter of choice influenced by social and religious background. There should be an acceptance of an ultimate creator source in all of us. It would surely be incongruous with the humanitarian compassion of healing not to believe in a compassionate creative God Source.

Divine Energy

Relevant to all healers is the attunement to a higher force to assist in the healing act. Philippine psychic surgeons insist that it requires the calling of the Holy Spirit to incorporate into them, charging the energy emanating from their hands to enable them to enter the patient's body. Harry Edwards, the great English spiritual healer, maintained it was *"the connecting spirit force between God and the healer. A healer must be correctly 'attuned' to enable spirit guides to work through him"* and that attunement is the connection between Man and his God to provide a channel for the flow of healing energies.

Truly great healers such as Joao Teixeira, Ze Arigo, Harry Edwards, and Edgar Cayce all maintain that it was not they who healed, but God. They believed, as most healers do, that they were only the vessel through whom the healing energies were passed.

Anecdote

In early 2001 I had the pleasure to meet with a lecturer from one of the most reputed Medical Universities in the USA. She was in Brazil seeking help from Joao de Deus for her own personal problems. For convenience let's call her Lisa. She told me a remarkable story.

She is a psychiatrist, respected for her holistic as well as her academic approach to her vocation. Even so, she was surprised when she was called to the office of the College Dean and asked to offer a short optional on the subject "Is There a Place for God in Modern Medicine." She was given just two hours for this subject!

To her amazement the thirty positions were over subscribed ten fold—almost three hundred people applied for the optional lecture.

On the first day she commenced the lecture by asking

everyone to write one paragraph on their thoughts about the subject. Then, before collecting them, she asked if anyone would like to give their view. The senior surgeon of the college rose and took the microphone. "I have never told anyone this but I feel compelled to tell you now. In all my years as a surgeon I never once took up a scalpel before I prayed to God to guide my hand."

The response from the class of medical students and faculty members was palpable. The façade of intellectual sophistication left every face and hands shot up across the auditorium in a spontaneous desire to air their personal beliefs.

Summary

- God is the supreme omnipotent intelligence and creative force that permeates all creation.

- God is spirit—a universal spiritual presence.

- We are all connected by a divine consciousness to all things.

- Within every living organism, including man, there is a fragment of the God consciousness.

- God is the healing force, the healer is the channel.

CHAPTER SIX

ANATOMY

"The simple transmission of life energy from one cell to another is the fundamental basis of all organic life forms, including the human body."
Dr Robert Becker.

It is imperative for any serious healer to have a basic knowledge of the physical and energetic makeup of the human body. Energy enters the body via particular channels and travels through glandular, circulatory, lymph and nervous systems, affecting organs and physiological structure at cellular level. Comprehension of these paths makes for easier presumption of the likely result. An appreciation of the functions of each of the major organs, glands and systems of the human body helps a visualisation of the action of the healing energy. It makes common sense to have an understanding of the body's structure and the interrelated functions of its components.

Body Pulsations

*"The human body is made up of electronic vibrations,
with each atom and element of the body, each organ
and organism having its electronic unit of vibration
necessary for the sustenance of, and equilibrium in,
that particular organism."*[23]

There are many synchronised rhythms at work within the
body. Medical science shows us that our body parts generate
rhythms from a high of 1000 hertz (1000 cycles per second) to a
low of 200 days per cycle. The brain is by far the fastest, generating
rapid electrical impulses (cerebral neurons) at 1000 Hz along the
nerve pathways. These impulses carry the signals that can switch
pain gates on or off when the body is threatened. The slower
cerebral rhythms, at around 50Hz, alternate in short bursts of
spike-like activity that convey our perception of change.

—**Beta rhythms**—generated in the frontal lobe of the brain,
  the beta rhythms of 14-28Hz are the wave activities
  emitted when we are in our normal awake state and are
  responsible for the more complex functions of
  judgement, personality and quick thinking.

—**Alpha rhythms**—7-14Hz, are produced as we drift into
  sleep or may be triggered consciously by meditation.
  Alpha is the relaxed, intuitive state where ideas are
  born. Alpha state is one of the most common semi-
  trance states engaged by healers. Most hypnosis takes
  place in the Alpha range.

—**Theta rhythms**—have a frequency of 4-7 Hz. This is a
  powerful range from which you can launch into a deep
  psychic experience.

—Delta rhythms—0-4Hz are generated on the surface of the brain. They mostly occur in the unconscious state. These rhythms are the power controllers that manipulate body functions.

Each organ has its own pulsation rate. The heart beats in two separate rhythms: the first chamber beats at around 76 per minute and the second at 40-90 per minute. The kidneys rise and fall in their secretion rate over a 24-hour cycle, shutting off the desire to secrete during the late evening until the early morning. Lungs move in and out every 3 seconds, controlled by the level of oxygen or carbon dioxide in the blood.

The rate of contraction of the stomach is about three times every minute, and the intestines move in a peristaltic contraction about once a minute.

Red blood cells each have a life of about 128 days. These are produced by the bone marrow and the bloodstream provides calcium salts needed to rebuild the bones every 200 days.

To a practiced healer each organ rhythm can often be "sensed" through the hands; the liver slow and sluggish, the pancreas fast, and the heart regular and steady. In a healthy body the rhythms are in synch, much like a well-rehearsed orchestra. Disease is felt when the body is not in rhythmic co-ordination. Much of the great results of energy healing are through the regulation of energy vibrations and pulsations of body components.

Glands

A gland is an organ or group of cells that secretes or excretes substances: mouth glands produce saliva; mammary glands excrete milk etc. Some glands are large organs such as the liver, pancreas and kidneys, but most are very tiny.

The Liver

The liver is the largest gland in the body and weighs about 1.5kg. Most of it lies behind the lower ribs on the right-hand side. The liver is the body's chemical processing plant. It regulates blood sugar levels, breaks down excess acids to be eliminated as urine, stores and modifies fats for more efficient use by body cells, nourishes new blood cells, stores certain vitamins and minerals, removes poisons from harmful substances such as alcohol and drugs, promotes new blood cells and destroys old cells and aids the digestive process by producing bile. The processing capabilities of the liver are amazingly complex and critical to the well being of the body. If the liver becomes diseased and cannot remove the yellow pigment bilirubin, a by-product of the destruction of old blood cells, the pigment stays in the blood and causes a yellow tinge to the skin and whites of the eyes—a quick tell-tale sign to be observed during consultation.

Note: During healing, the liver's response to directly applied energy can be felt and even heard quite audibly after only a few minutes of application.

The Spleen

Despite the generally accepted medical opinion that the spleen is not an essential organ, according to esoteric beliefs it is in fact the *"gateway from the auric body to the physical body through which the energies of light enter."* [24] The spleen is a ductless gland connected by a portal vein to the liver. A portal vein has no valve, so blood can flow both ways to and from the liver. The spleen also manufactures the white corpuscles in the blood. It is about as big a man's clenched fist and is located in the abdominal area under the lower left ribs.

The Kidneys

The kidneys lay either side of the spine just above the waist. Their main function is to filter the blood to remove impurities and waste products. They ensure various elements of our blood such as proteins, salts, vitamins and nutrients remain balanced. They also regulate the balance of fluid in the body—if the body is short of fluid they return more water to the bloodstream, if there is excess fluid they pass it out as urine.

About a litre of blood is pumped into the kidneys every minute, the entire blood stream is purified every 50 minutes.

The Endocrine Glands

Endocrine glands are glands without ducts and are enormously important in the functioning of the human body. They secrete hormones directly into the bloodstream, which act as chemical messages that regulate and balance vital processes in the body. Amongst other functions, they influence our growth, metabolism and sexual development. (See fig. 2)

The major endocrine glands are:

- PITUITARY—located in the centre of the skull behind the "third eye,"

- PINEAL—between the ears, at the centre of the skull,

- THYROID—in the front lower neck, just below the Adams Apple,

- THYMUS—just below the thyroid gland,

- ADRENALS—situated on the top of the kidneys,

- PANCREAS—sitting just behind the stomach, and

- OVARIES and the TESTES.

Endocrine glands work in conjunction with each other, so that the release of hormones in one gland will influence the operation of a different gland.

The endocrine system is of the utmost importance to the energy healer. A quote from an old book on esoteric healing gives some indication of how energies, entering the system via the chakras, affect the body through the endocrine glandular connections. *"They (the incoming energies) work directly upon the physical body through the medium of the endocrine system. This point should be borne in mind by all healers. He (the healer) will work through those centres (chakras) and glands which govern the particular area of the body wherein the disease or discomfort is located.*"It also indicates how external pressures, entering via the same centre, can affect the endocrine system and bring disease to the body; *"Agitation in the etheric body, any violent activity under stress, temper, intense worry or prolonged irritation will pour a stream of astral energy into and through the solar plexus centre, and will galvanise that centre into a condition of intense disturbance. This affects the stomach, spleen, pancreas, gall duct and bladder."*[25]

The endocrine system is a vital focal point for healing by introduction of healing energies through the seven primary energy centres (chakras), particularly those in the solar plexus area and the head.

Pituitary Gland

Of all endocrine glands the most influential on the entire body is the *pituitary*. Often referred to as *the master gland of the endocrine system*, it not only has its own functions but regulates other glands too. Altogether, this gland produces nine different hormones. Some stimulate the thyroid, some the adrenal glands, another acts on the kidneys and regulates the balance of water and salts in body fluids, while others affect our growth.

The pituitary gland is responsible for the production of sex hormones and mother's nursing milk. During birth it stimulates the uterus muscles to propel the child through the birth canal. The direct connection of the pituitary gland via the hypothalamus to the brain and the entire nervous system is why this gland plays such an important role in mental and physical wellbeing. If the pituitary gland malfunctions, the effects can be wide-ranging because of the gland's influence on so many parts of the body.

Direct energy stimulation of the pituitary gland is of the utmost importance during healing input. Energy applied to the forehead and base of the skull and directed to the pituitary can prompt a remarkable regulatory effect on the body through energy stimulation of the endocrinal glandular system.

Thyroid

Situated at the front of the throat just below the Adam's apple the thyroid consists of two wings, one on either side of the windpipe. Its function is to control the rate at which the body converts food to energy as well as the rate of growth in adolescence. To carry out these functions the thyroid produces two hormones that contain iodine— essential for correct metabolism. Too much iodine and the metabolism speeds up resulting in hyperactivity, sleeplessness, tremors, palpitations and emotional disturbances. Too little and the reverse occurs: coldness, tiredness and constipation.

Thymus

The thymus, located on the trachea below the thyroid, produces antibodies and white blood cells to fight against infection. The thymus, tonsils and spleen are part of the lymphatic system.

The Pancreas

This large gland is located in the middle of the abdomen just above the navel. The pancreas has two roles; producing insulin for the control of the body's use of sugar, and to produce juices and enzymes used in the digestion of food, squirting them on to the food as it passes from the stomach into the small intestine.

Hypothalamus & Pineal Glands

The hypothalamus is the *master controller* of the body. It acts like the chief executive officer of the organism, passing on orders from the brain to the rest of the body and ensuring that they are carried out. The hypothalamus coordinates and regulates most of our life-sustaining functions. A little recognised fact is the vital effect of light and colour on the hypothalamus; when light and colour enter the eye's 130 million photoreceptors they are transmitted along several different routes that involve the entire brain: some to the *visual cortex* and some to the *hypothalamus, pituitary gland* and its associate, the *pineal* gland.

As the body's major collection centre for information concerned with its well being, the hypothalamus receives all *external information* picked up by our sense organs and all *internal signals* from the autonomic nervous system as well as from the *psyche*. Its major functions include control of the autonomic nervous system, energy balance, heat regulation, activity and sleep, circulation, breathing, growth, reproduction and emotional balance. **Thus, the hypothalamus may well be the single most important unit of the brain as the high command in maintaining harmony within the body.**

Information received by the hypothalamus is also used to control the secretions of the pituitary gland, thereby affecting the body's other major regulatory system—the endocrine glandular system. Now that the connection between the eyes, the hypothalamus, the autonomic nervous system and the endocrine system have been established, the importance of their reaction to light/colour/energy stimulation cannot be overstated in seeking to bring about harmony to body functions.

The Pineal Gland

Rene Descartes described the pineal as the *"seat of the soul."* Intuitively understood by the ancients, greatly underestimated by modern science, the pineal serves to assist us in bonding with the universe. Located under the lower rear portion of the brain, it is connected to, what is referred to in Indian culture and Yoga practice, as the "third eye." The pineal's activity, regulated by environmental light changes and Earth's electromagnetic field, transmits information to the body, pertaining to the length of daylight and hence the forthcoming seasons. In this way it maintains our body's attunement to nature, adjusting our physiology for upcoming environmental changes. Shaped like a miniature pinecone, sculptures of the pineal can be seen all over ancient Europe, usually at gateways, an indication perhaps that there is a great deal more to this small pea-sized gland than modern science understands.

The Lymphatic System

All cells in the body are surrounded by fluid that is fed with oxygen and nutrients from the bloodstream. As well as being maintained at active levels, this fluid must be constantly removed, otherwise it would accumulate in the tissues. Some of it is removed via the blood stream and some through the lymphatic system. The lymphatics consist of minute capillaries (very narrow vessels with extra thin walls) leading into progressively larger lymphatic channels that eventually unite to form two big ducts, emptying into veins at the base of the neck—thus returning the fluid to the bloodstream. The lymphatic system compliments the circulatory system (See fig 3).

The colourless fluid that is filtered into the lymphatic capillaries is somewhat similar to blood plasma but with a different chemical composition. Along the vast network of lymphatic vessels are tiny lymph nodes (glands). These are miniature bead-like structures that filter out germs and poisons from the lymph liquid. They also produce lymph cells, a type of white blood cell, and antibodies to destroy harmful substances. There are especially high concentrations of lymph glands in the armpits, groin and neck, which may become noticeably swollen and painful when an infection is present due to stepped up production of antibodies.

Unlike the circulatory system, there is no pump to keep the lymph liquid moving along the ducts, but a network of valves exist to prevent the liquid from draining backwards. Circulation of lymph liquid is maintained partly by the pressure as it is forced through the capillary walls, but also as a result of breathing, muscle contraction and body movement. Regular exercise is therefore very important in maintaining proper lymph circulation.

The lymphatic network also includes three large glands: the *tonsils*, the *spleen* and the *thymus*. Each of these glands produces antibodies to fight off infection. It is not hard to see why particular attention should be paid to applying energy to the predominant lymph areas of the neck, the groin and the front shoulders near the armpits, as well as to the three major lymph glands. Patients should be encouraged to take regular exercise such as a brisk walk to ensure a healthy circulation of lymph fluids.

Cardiovascular System

Blood is life—symbolically and factually. Blood is pumped by the heart along a complex network of narrow channels. The blood vessels carrying blood out to the tissues from the heart are called *arteries*. Those carrying blood back to the heart are called *veins*. Linking small veins and small arteries are tiny transparent vessels called *capillaries*, which allow the exchange of fluids between blood and body cells and between blood and air in the lungs.

All cells in the body are immersed in a salty liquid called *tissue fluid*. It is this fluid that makes possible the exchange of all substances necessary to keep the cells alive and all the waste products that must be discarded after the life-giving substances have been utilised. There are two main circuits of blood vessels. Those carrying blood between the heart and the lungs for oxygenation are called the *pulmonary vessels*. The arteries and veins supplying the rest of the body with food and oxygen are called the *systemic vessels*.

Blood cells are nourished by protein in a complex process. DNA molecules provide patterns for shaping RNA ribonucleic acid molecules, which in turn provide patterns for the making of protein. Each kind of protein molecule is built from a complicated chain of energies with thousands of amino acid groups linked in a precise order. Where cells are deprived of correct nutrients, proteins, and oxygen by failure of the vascular system to transport these life-sustaining elements throughout the body, illness occurs resulting in physical debility, lack of vitality, fatigue and instability of function. Introducing healing energies to the cardiovascular system re-energises blood cells and encourage an improved state in the molecular structure to the patient's benefit.

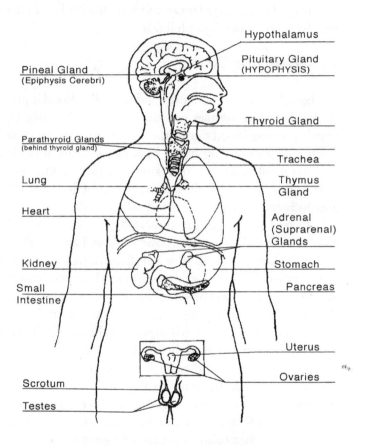

Hypothalamus

Pineal Gland
(Epiphysis Cerebri)

Pituitary Gland
(HYPOPHYSIS)

Thyroid Gland

Parathyroid Glands
(behind thyroid gland)

Trachea

Lung

Thymus Gland

Heart

Adrenal (Suprarenal) Glands

Kidney

Stomach

Small Intestine

Pancreas

Uterus

Ovaries

Scrotum

Testes

Location of endocrine glands

Fig. 2

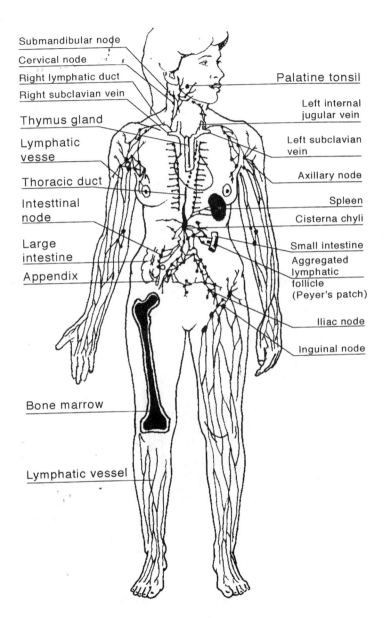

Submandibular node
Cervical node
Right lymphatic duct
Right subclavian vein
Thymus gland
Lymphatic vesse
Thoracic duct
Intesttinal node
Large intestine
Appendix

Palatine tonsil
Left internal jugular vein
Left subclavian vein
Axillary node
Spleen
Cisterna chyli
Small intestine
Aggregated lymphatic follicle (Peyer's patch)
Iliac node
Inguinal node

Bone marrow

Lymphatic vessel

Lymphatic system: principle components

Fig. 3

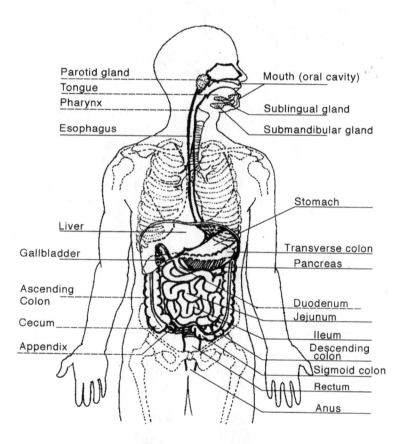

Parotid gland

Tongue

Pharynx

Esophagus

Mouth (oral cavity)

Sublingual gland

Submandibular gland

Stomach

Liver

Transverse colon

Gallbladder

Pancreas

Ascending
Colon

Duodenum

Cecum

Jejunum

Ileum

Appendix

Descending
colon

Sigmoid colon

Rectum

Anus

Organs of the digestive system

Fig. 4

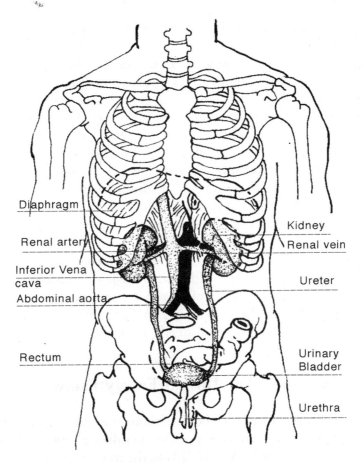

Diaphragm

Renal artery

Inferior Vena cava

Abdominal aorta

Rectum

Kidney

Renal vein

Ureter

Urinary Bladder

Urethra

Urinary System: male organs

Fig. 5

The Nervous System

This complicated network of cells enables all parts of the body to communicate with the brain and with each other to bring about bodily activity. The brain is the centre of the nervous system, and together with the spinal cord forms what is called the *nervous system*. The remaining nerves form the *peripheral nervous system*.

There are two networks of nerves. One is under conscious control. This we use for physical activities to enable us to move our legs when we want to walk or move our arms for balance. The other network is unconscious and operates irrespective of any conscious control on our part. This network is called the *autonomic nervous system* and is responsible for such bodily functions as breathing and digestion.

The autonomic system, in turn, is divided into two—the *sympathetic* and the *parasympathetic* system. The sympathetic system stimulates activity and the parasympathetic system stops or slows activity down.

Broadly speaking, the nervous system receives messages through receptors in the skin and throughout the body that record sensations such as heat, cold, balance, heartbeat, pain and others. This is called the *sensitory system*. Responses to these inward messages are then transmitted to the muscles and glands of the motor system.

Meridians—The Unseen Energy Pathways

There are various schools of thought explaining the action of acupuncture stimulation of the meridian pathways. Classical references date back to 100BC in the recordings of Nei Jing. In Ling Shu, chapter 8, the theory of a connection with spirit is expounded; *"for every needling, the method is above all, not to miss the rooting in the spirit."*[26] This ancient book maintains that acupuncture is really a method of attunement of the body, nature and universal essence to bring about a holistic harmony and balance between these elements. This theory stood for more than 2000 years until western medicine looked for a more scientific explanation.

In 1971, medical scientist Robert Becker conducted a series of experiments to test the theory that acupuncture meridians *"were electrical conductors that carried an injury message to the brain, which responded by sending back the appropriate level of direct current to stimulate healing in the troubled area."*[27] The tests measured the flow of electrical current in the perineural cells just under the skin and indicated that each acupuncture point along the way was electrically positive compared to its environs, and each one had a field surrounding it with its own characteristic pattern. Later tests isolated the interfering reaction of the nerves along the route thus indicating that the response was carried, not by the nerves themselves, but by the underlying perineural sleeve.

So what does all this mean to a bio-energy healer? The ancient text supports our belief that energy healing input is holistic and requires the involvement of spirit—*"we must input to the spirit."* The Becker experiments show us *how* the energy impulses are transmitted along the meridians and how the brain triggers a healing or pain-calming response.

Healers will immediately recognise that this accounts for the fact that it is not always necessary to apply energy directly to the afflicted area. Often the treatment can be applied elsewhere along the energy meridian. Applied, for example, to the upper left foot above the big toe or to the inside left leg adjacent to the knee, will supply energy to the liver.

Reflexologists too utilise the body's meridian connections to stimulate organs via a corresponding point on the sole of the foot. Thus, in energy healing, energy applied to the sole of the foot will travel to the appropriate location within the body.

There is, of course, a great deal more to human anatomy than this but the above are the basic pre-requisites for any energy therapist. You should continue to study and expand your knowledge of the miracle of the human body and its response to energy healing input.

Anecdote

In Florence, Italy in 1997, my then wife, who is an energy healer, emerged fron her clinic room at the end of a long day of patients with tears in her eyes. "I have cancer," she said. " A tumour on the liver in the upper left lobe. Under the rib cage."

A flurry of scans, MRIs and blood tests supported her worst fears. Doctors wanted to operate immediately. It was a fast growing type and the sooner they removed it the better, they insisted. But she was not going to be rushed into radical surgery. Much to their disapproval, she opted for Brazil and Joao de Deus instead.

She knew the risks. She could feel the tumour growing, spreading rapidly as it fed on the blood vessels and nutrients of the liver. Within days it was pressing against the rib cage. There was no time to loose. Unfortunately we couldn't get to Brazil for five weeks. During this time we were increasingly alarmed at its rate of growth.

On our eventual arrival at the centre she went immediately to Joao-in-Entity and asked for a physical operation. "No, my sister," he said, "just sit there in the current and I will operate."

She did as she was told and sat in meditation in the current (a room full of mediums all generating energy in meditation). Some forty minutes later she felt twinges and heat around the area. When her head began to feel dizzy she asked to lie down and was removed to a hospital type ward to rest. Two months later new scans, blood tests and MRI show no sign of cancer and she has been free of any resurgence for more than eight years.

Summary

- The simple transmission of life energy from one cell to another is the fundamental basis of all organic life forms, including the human body.

- Energy enters the body via particular channels and travels through glandular, circulatory, lymph and nervous systems affecting organs and physiological structure at cellular level.

- The healer should have an understanding of energy entry points and pathways and the groups of organs affected by each entry gateway.

- The human body is made up of electronic vibrations, each atom and element of the body, each organ and organism having its electronic unit of vibration necessary for the sustenance of, and equilibrium in, that particular organism.

- The liver is the body's chemical processing plant. It regulates blood sugar, breaks down excess acids, stores and modifies fats, nourishes new blood cells, stores certain vitamins and minerals, removes poisons from such harmful substances as alcohol and drugs, promotes new blood cells, destroys old cells and aids the digestive process by producing bile.

- The spleen is a major gateway from the auric body to the physical body through which energies enter.

- The kidneys filter the blood to remove impurities and waste products, ensure various elements of our blood such as proteins, salts, vitamins and nutrients remain balanced, and regulate the balance of fluid in the body.

- Endocrine glands are glands without ducts and are enormously important in the functioning of the human body. They secrete hormones directly into the bloodstream, which act as chemical messages that regulate and balance vital processes in the body. Amongst other functions, they influence our growth, metabolism and sexual development.

- The endocrine system is a vital focal point for introduction of healing energies through the seven primary energy centres (chakras), particularly those in the solar plexus area and the head.

- The pituitary gland is the master gland of the endocrine system. It not only has its own functions but regulates other glands too. Energy applied to the pituitary area affects all other glands in the endocrine system.

- The pancreas has two roles; producing insulin for the control of the body's use of sugar, and to produce the juices used in the digestion of food.

- The hypothalamus is the master controller of the body. It coordinates and regulates most of our life-sustaining functions including control of the autonomic nervous system, energy balance, heat regulation, activity and sleep, circulation, breathing, growth, reproduction, and emotional balance. Thus, the hypothalamus may well be the single most important unit of the brain as the high command in maintaining harmony within the body.

- The pineal gland is known as the *"seat of the soul"*.

- The colourless fluid filtered into the lymphatic capillaries is similar to blood plasma, but with a different chemical composition. Along the vast network of lymphatic vessels are tiny lymph nodes, miniature bead-like structures that filter out germs and poisons from the lymph liquid. They also produce lymph cells (a type of white blood cell) and antibodies to destroy harmful substances.

- Meridians transverse the entire body, delivering energy impulses along unseen pathways to induce a healing or pain-calming response.

CHAPTER SEVEN

THE HUMAN ENERGY FIELD

Mind does not work directly on the brain. There is an etheric body link between mind and the cells of the brain. Far more minute corpuscular (life force) particles than scientists are yet aware of travel along threads from the etheric body to certain regions of the body and the brain. The invisible etheric body is the only channel through which mind and life may communicate with the physical body. Every living thing has a unifying invisible body made out of modified ether.

Geraldine Cummins—Medium 1930

The physical body has an energy counterpart referred to by many names: ethereal body, aura, energy field, bio-energy field, human energy field (HEF). The human energy field and the physical body are interactive with each other. When either one is in a state of ill health, the other appears dull and lacklustre. An understanding of their interrelationship is invaluable for successful therapeutic treatment.

Historical Research

In the early 19th century, scientific discoveries in electro magnetics led to the concept of a *field*. A field was defined as *a condition in space, which has the potential of producing a force.* Further research resulted in the concept of a universe filled with fields that create forces that interact with each other. This was later supported in the 1800s by mathematician Helmont, who visualized *a universal fluid—a pure vital spirit that pervades all nature and penetrates all bodies.*

Another important discovery was Einstein's theory that matter and energy were interchangeable. Mass is a form of energy, which has slowed down and crystallized. Thus our bodies are simply condensed energy. Hence it is often referred to as "the gross material body."

These two accepted concepts are the scientific basis of energy healing. Our bodies are condensed energies surrounded by and interacting with a vibrant energy field known as the Human Energy Field (HEF). This vital energy, perceived as a vibrant luminous body, was first recorded in western literature by the Pythagoreans around 500 BC. They held that its light could produce a variety of effects in the human organism, including the cure of illness.

In 1911, Dr. William Kilner observed the HEF through coloured screens and filters as three layers; a quarter inch dark layer close to the body; a vaporous layer an inch wide streaming perpendicularly from the body, and a delicate exterior luminosity about six inches across. This he called the "aura". He observed that it differed in subjects depending on age, sex, mental state and health. Certain diseases showed as patches or irregularities in the aura, which led him to develop a system of diagnosis on the basis of the colour, texture, volume and general appearance of the field.

In the 1930s Drs Lawrence and Phobe Bendit made extensive scientific observations of the HEF and related the fields to health, healing and soul development. Their work stresses the importance of the powerful etheric forces that are the foundations of health and healing in the human body. These observations revealed a vital energy field that forms a matrix interpenetrating the dense physical body like a sparkling web of light beams. This energetic matrix is the basic pattern upon which the physical matter of the tissues is shaped and anchored.

These observations are supported by the work of Professor William A. Tiller, Department of Material Science, Stanford University, who wrote; *"There are different levels of substance, each of a different configuration. They obey entirely different laws and they have unique characteristics of radiation (absorption and emission). They operate in different kinds of space-time frames in the universe and so are distinct from each other. These levels are:*

- *the physical*
- *the etheric*
- *astral level*
- *three levels of mind*
  - ○ *Instinctive mind*
  - ○ *Intellectual mind, and*
  - ○ *Spiritual mind*
- *spirit. "*

Professor Tiller believed there exists another level called the *Divine* from which the holographic blueprint for all created matter comes. The hologram for the human body is carried in the auric layers as the pattern for the physical body. When the body is subjected to disharmony or abnormal mind patterns, not consistent with the initial pattern, disease results first within the energy fields and then the disharmony is projected into the physical body. His theory is consistent with many esoterical writings.

More recently, researcher Dr Karagulla compared the aura observations of sensitives (clairvoyants) to known physical disorders of ill patients and concluded that sensitives could indeed "see" irregularities in the ethereal body, which coincided with medical prognosis. The sensitives were able to detect and describe accurately what the medical problems were, from brain disorders to obstruction of the colon.

It is now generally accepted that when the vital human energy field is healthy, there is within it a natural autonomous rhythm in which each organ of the body has its own corresponding energetic rhythm within the etheric field. Between the spheres of the various organs the different rhythms interact as if a transfer function were occurring. When the body is whole and healthy these rhythms transfer easily from organ to organ. In illness the energy rhythms and patterns are changed so that there is an irregularity between them, resulting in energy dissipation or accumulation rather than an easy flow through all tissue.

The HEF is a combination of scientifically measurable components: electrostatic, magnetic, electromagnetic, sonic, thermal and visual aspects that are consistent with the physiological processes of the human body. Measurements show definite frequencies for each different colour layer of the aura. They also show it to be fluid in motion and made of subatomic particles that, when charged, move together in clouds know as *plasmas*. Plasmas follow certain physical laws, which scientists believe to be a state between energy and matter. The term *bioplasma* is used to specifically refer to plasmas of the human body. However, a human energy field defined simply as an electromagnetic field is insufficient as it does not explain the irrefutable evidence of psychic phenomena associated with the HEF, such as precognition, past life awareness, ESP, clairvoyance, and clairaudience. It is now considered by many that the HEF is *the memory store of all past experiences, knowledge and spiritual awareness, contrary to the popular belief that these are stored in the physical brain.*

The aura (HEF) can now be described as *the bioplasmic ethereal body surrounding and penetrating the human form. It is the physical, emotional and spiritual protective field from which most illnesses are either defeated or accumulate to the lower density of the physical body.* Conversely, *the aura also reflects the condition of the physical body.* If the body is in disease the aura will be dull and lacking in vitality. Some people can see the aura but most cannot. Some "see" it clairvoyantly or intuitively.

The Seven Auric Layers

The HEF comprises seven layers encompassing the body. Each layer has its own frequency and hence its own colour. Each is connected via a chakra, invisible spinning vortexes of energy, to the physical body. Each chakra shares the same frequency and colour as its auric layer and is the "funnel" through which energy is conducted to and from a specific area of influence of the body (Fig 6).

The seven layers are divided into three lower and three upper groups plus the final seventh. The lower three layers, closest to the body, are associated with the *physical world*. The upper three layers metabolise energies related to the *spiritual world*. The fourth layer, the dividing band between the two groups, is the astral level and is associated with the *heart chakra* through which all energies must pass in transit from one group and one reality to another. In other words, spiritual energy must pass through the heart process to be transformed to physical energy and conversely, physical energy will transform to spiritual as it exits through the heart chakra. Interestingly, many religious paintings depict Christ holding a flaming heart.

The seventh layer is the divine connection to the Creative Consciousness.

The Lower Three Layers

The First Layer (Ethereal Body)

The ethereal layer lies closest to the body and is the energy matrix within which the body tissues are first formed prior to manifestation in the physical form (remembering that all cells of the body are constantly renewed in a cycle of approximately 180 days). It has the same structure as the physical body including all the anatomical parts and organs. Thus this energy field sets up the matrix in the shape of the body parts prior to their cellular growth in their ultimate physical form. The matrix is formed before the cells materialize physically.

Just 1cm to 5cm in width, light blue to grey in colour, it is composed of a sparkling web of energy lines upon which the physical matter of the body tissues is shaped and anchored. It has a rippling action as it pulsates in a flowing motion around the body at approx. 15-20 cycles per minute.

The Second Layer (Emotional Body)

This layer is associated with emotions and feelings. It follows the outline of the physical body and penetrates the ethereal field. It comprises all the colours of the rainbow in coloured clouds of fine substances, which are in constant fluid motion. Colours become clearer and more vivid when influenced by highly energized feelings such as love, excitement, joy or anger. Confused and depressive feelings tend to muddy and darken the hue.

The Third Layer (Mental Body)

The third aura body is associated with thoughts and the mental processes. Appearing predominantly as a bright yellow light radiating about the head and shoulders, it extends around the whole body. It extends and brightens as the owner concentrates on mental processes. Thought forms appear as blobs of bright yellow with additional coloured hues emanating from the emotional layer. Habitual thoughts tend to become more permanent and affect our lives and our belief system to a marked degree.

The Upper Four Layers

The Fourth Layer (Astral Body)

The heart is the key to all. Through this layer, and its associated chakra, filter all energies, thoughts and experiences, which ultimately affect us emotionally, physically and spiritually. Composed of coloured clouds more beautiful than the emotional body, it is infused with the rose colour of love. This is the dividing band between the lower and upper groups. It is associated with the heart chakra through which all energies must pass in transit from one group of layers and from one reality to another. In other words, spiritual energy must pass through the heart process to be transformed to physical energy and conversely, physical energy will transform to spiritual as it exits through the heart chakra. It extends 10cm to 30cm from the body.

A great deal of interaction takes place between people on this astral level. Clouds of colour stretch out across a room between people, some pleasant, some not, with the result that you may feel uneasy about someone you are not even talking to. There can be a colourful bonding interaction between two people who have never met. Barbara Brennan, in *"Hands of Light"*, claims she can observe lots of energy forms exchanging between a man and a woman fantasizing lovemaking. She claims there is *"an actual testing in the energy fields to see if the fields are synchronous and if the people are compatible."* She also states that; *"when people form relationships, they grow cords out of the aura fields, through the chakras that connect them. The longer the relationship, the more chords and the stronger they are. When the relationship ends these chords are torn, often causing a great deal of pain" (heartache) until they disconnect and reroute within the self."*

Fifth Layer (Template Body)

This layer contains all the forms that exist on the physical plane in a template or blueprint form, like a negative. Hence it is known as the template body. It projects this template of the body to the etheric layer (first layer) where body tissues are then materialised on the grid matrix upon which the physical body grows. It extends from 45cm to 60cm from the body.

When distortion in the etheric layer is detected work is necessary in the template layer to provide support for the etheric layer in its original template form.

To the attuned healer the template form contains the entire structure of the auric field, including chakras, body organs and body forms in a negative blueprint format. This layer connects physical reality with other realities.

Sixth Layer (Celestial Body)

The sixth is the emotional level of the spiritual plane called the *celestial body.*

It is the level through which we experience spiritual ecstasy. We can reach it through meditation and other forms of transformation. It is from here we can reach a point of "being" where we know our connection with all the universe—immerse in the Light and feel we are of it, and it of us—we are at one with God.

When the open celestial chakra is connected with the open heart chakra we experience unconditional love, of all humanity, of humans in the flesh and of spiritual love that goes beyond the physical to all realms of reality.

The sixth layer extends from 60cm-80cm from the body in a shimmering opalescent pastel light. It appears to radiate out from the body like the glow around a candle.

The Seventh Layer (Ketheric Body)

This is the mental level of the spiritual plane—it extends 80cm-100cm from the body. The outer form is egg shape extending out beyond the body by 100cm with the smaller tip beneath the feet and the larger end about 100cm above the head.

It comprises a shimmering light of golden silver threads, pulsating at very high frequency that holds the whole auric form together. It has a thin protective layer on the outside rather like an eggshell, which protects the enclosed fields.

This golden field supplies the main power current that runs up and down the spine and nourishes the entire body. As this current, introduced through the crown chakra, pulsates up and down the spine it carries energy, which connects to the energies carried into the body by the other six chakras.

It contains all of the auric bodies associated with the present incarnation of the individual. When we bring our consciousness to the seventh level we are at one with the Creato.[28]

The Chakras

The chakras are spinning vortexes of energy that pull energy into the body from the environment and distribute then within your body. Each is connected to its corresponding energy layer and provides energy, light and colour to its region of influence within the body. Although the seven primary chakras are those normally referred to, there are many other minor chakras throughout the body such as those in the palms of the hands. Each chakra is paired with its counterpart on the back but they are in fact the one chakra. The frontal aspects are related to feelings and the rear to the will.

The Base Chakra

The Base, or Root, Chakra sits at the bottom of the spine, spinning over the sexual organs and pelvis. It carries life energies up into the body, through the other chakras, as well as down the legs. This chakra is the "grounding" connection to the Earth's subtle energies and through it we know our identity with the Earth and our origins.

Some spiritual concepts are misguided because they assume

that the base chakra becomes less important as our spirituality grows—this is not so. The base chakra is as spiritually relevant as the higher chakras. In it is stored our ancestral relationships, childhood and past life material thus it can be a storehouse for past traumas. It is the chakra wherein our desires to satisfy sexual needs arises. The Base Chakra is most often associated with the colour red, but this is not always the case as other colours can be seen in the chakra in response to different influences.

The Second Chakra

Also known as the Abdominal Chakra because of its location over the lower abdominal area, from the top of the pelvic bone to the belly button. This chakra is the seat of creation. It covers the small and large intestine; it is here the nourishment from food is extracted for cell development and growth. It is also responsible for the womb, fallopian tubes and ovaries in which the creation of life is spawned. It is here that the body embraces the soul. The second chakra reveals the affection and compassion of the soul—the essence within. Most caring and dedicated healers have a strong and active second chakra.

The Third Chakra

The Solar Plexus Chakra, located between the belly button and the lower rib cage, covers more organs than any other chakra. On the left side are the spleen, pancreas and stomach. On the right side are the liver and gall bladder and to the rear the kidneys and adrenals. In the upper area lies the diaphragm, which expels used energy. Often when healing the diaphram works overtime "vacuuming" the dead energies from the client, expelling it in rushes of air like a huge uncontrollable yawn.

"Each organ's function in your body parallels its role in your emotional life. Consider the organs within the third chakra. As the filtering system that detects toxins in your bloodstream, the kidneys are your prototype for fear and caution, for detecting and eliminating that which is dangerous. As a factory that breaks down whatever is harmful to your system, your liver is your prototype for self-protective anger. As the alarm system that triggers great rushes of energy for emergencies, the adrenals are the prototype for the panic response that mobilizes you in a crisis. As the body's producer of metabolic juices, the pancreas is the prototype for assimilating what you can embrace. As the organ that sends stale air out of your body, the diaphragm is the prototype for grieving and finding closure with whatever is passing out of our life."[29]

The Fourth Chakra

This is the Heart Chakra that has within its area of influence the heart, lungs, thymus, and pericardium—a protective sac that surrounds the heart. The heart chakra is the middle chakra and the middle colour of the spectrum—green—but other colours may be evident. When the heart chakra emits a golden hue it is usually an indication that the person has a universal love that attracts people to them. A soft pink hue is evident in those who are loving, kind and soft.

In these days of fierce competition many heart chakras are underdeveloped because people are guided more by their head than by their heart. Conversely it is unhealthy to have a heart chakra that is too large. These people tend to "care too much," taking on everyone's pain and problems to their own detriment, in this case it is desirable to build up the other chakras so there is more balance within the entire energy system.

The heart chakra is the center through which all energies must pass in transit from one group of layers, and from one reality to another. This chakra and its associated layer, filters all energies, thoughts and experience that ultimately affect us emotionally, physically and spiritually. The heart chakra is the central focus between the lower and upper groups.

The Fifth Chakra

Through the Throat Chakra, whose areas of influence include the thyroid and parathyroid glands, all energies and information are disseminated as they pass to and from the higher seventh and sixth chakras to the lower heart, third, second and base chakras. This is the filtering point for all data that is sorted, systemized and then dispersed as our personal expression. Just as the thyroid breaks down food for the body it also breaks down the energies that pass through it to maintain the energy body. All energies that flow up and down the meridians of the body pass through this area.

The colour normally found in the throat chakra is turquoise.

The Sixth Chakra

The area of influence for the Forehead Chakra covers eyes, ears, lower area of the brain cortex, pituitary gland, and the "director of bodily operations," the hypothalamus. It is within the brain cortex that we are able to calculate, plan and perform abstract mental operations that enable us to transcend the physical body—travelling to the future, past, the imagined, and access to symbols, meanings, theories, and fantasies. It is via the sixth chakra that we are able to access the psychic plane and traverse the dimensions of time and space. Modern thinking, intellect, and busy minds tend to dominate the more subtle but powerful connections to the psychic, which are the channels we use to receive guidance and subtle energies beyond our ordinary perception. This is not so prevalent in non-western cultures where more subtle ways of "knowing" are not crowded out by dense academic and commercial preoccupation.

This chakra is referred to as the third eye, which many cultures associate with psychic development. Located in the centre of the forehead just above the eyebrows and the bridge of the nose it acts much like an eye but the vision appears in the mind, as if viewing through an invisible funnel or a circle of white haze. A simple method of sensing the third eye is to close your eyes and hold the palm of your right hand over it but not quite touching your forehead. Within sixty seconds the palm heats up, at two minutes remove your hand and feel the residue energy continue. It will feel alive for an hour or more.

The Seventh Chakra

The Crown Chakra is our spiritual connection to the cosmos, the divine link to "all that is", the oneness of creation and God. It is the integration of personality with life, which gives the person a sense of purpose to their existence. It relates to the whole being, physical, mental, spiritual, and emotional—a holistic state of balance.

Relationship of Chakras and Endocrine Glands

The endocrine glands are located throughout the analogous circuitry of the seven primary chakras. That is to say each chakra disperses energy to its associated endocrine gland. It is no coincident that the chakras and the endocrine glands are within the same spatial location throughout the body. In figure 7, we see the location of the various chakras and the glands and organs located within each area of influence corresponding to that chakra.

There is an inductive coupling between the etheric body and the physical body that produces a variety of energy currents into the physical body and a reverse flow out of the body into the etheric body, and out into the environment.

We can see from figure 6, the interconnectedness of the primary chakra network to the seven layers of the human energy field. Figure 8 shows the side view of the chakras with their respective psychoenergetic association to the spine and hence the nervous system. Chakras are located central to their areas of influence. Their root stems are closely related to the endocrine system, and their nerve and cardiovascular systems.

This correlation of chakras to endocrine glands and organs is important in energy healing. **Energy introduced at each chakra location will have an effect on the corresponding glands and their network of nerves, organs and vessels within that area of influence.** This in some way explains why many ancient healing texts say that the most important entry point for healing of the body is the solar plexus chakra, perhaps because its area of influence is so large and contains so many major organs.

1. Base chakra: ovaries and testes

2. Abdominal chakra: intestines, bladder, womb, fallopian tubes

3. Solar plexus chakra: spleen, kidneys, liver, adrenals, stomach, gallbladder, pancreas

4. Heart chakra: heart, lungs, pericardium

5. Throat chakra: thyroid, parathyroid, thymus

6. Head chakra: hypothalamus, pineal, pituitary, lower brain cortex, eyes

7. Crown chakra: divine connection

Energy Healing—Auric or Physical?

There is a great deal of confusion in the various disciplines of energy healing as to whether the patient should be treated via the *bio-energy fields* or by *direct contact* with the physical body? There are three schools of thought on this question:

- Healing only through the aura and chakras.
- Healing by direct contact with the body, or
- A combination of both.

A combination of both is the preferred option of most healers with a preference for direct body application supported by additional vitality enhancement through the energy fields.

Each therapist will develop his/her own technique, applying healing energies by the method they find most responsive. Once the therapist accepts Spiritual Healing in its full context however, this problem is no longer perplexing because the application of the energies will be decided and directed by Spirit, as and where required, to achieve the desired effect.

The HEF contains the energy building blocks and the blueprint matrix plan for construction and maintenance of the denser material form—the physical body. It should be remembered that bio-energy fields and the physical body interact and respond to each other. *When one is out of sorts the other reflects the state of its counterpart.* Therefore it is possible to treat one for an effect in the other. Thus some strands of healing arts prefer to treat the ailment through the energy fields, whilst others recommend inputting to the body directly.

Auras change as our moods change. The mind of the HEF and the mind of the physical person are linked. Therefore, our thoughts affect our aura. It could be said that our aura is a mirror of our soul, our inner self, and our life energy. Thus the aura reflects the personality of the soul; loving, caring, kind, compassionate or bad tempered, complaining, selfish. How vitally important it is then, for the therapist to encourage self-help from the patient during consultation; coaxing a happier and more pleasant disposition to bring about a healthier mindset, which ultimately reflects in a stronger and more vibrant life force.

If a malady exits within the body, it will distort its counterpart in the energy matrix. Conversely, if the energy matrix is distorted it will project ill health into the body.

Primarily, healing by energy application is achieved via the human energy field.

Anecdote

Evidence that the human energy field (aura) protects our physical body is difficult to prove. One incident in Brazil, in March 1998, clearly demonstrated the effects when this protection is weakened.

There is a rule at the healing centre in Abadiania: do not enter the current rooms for twenty-four hours after any operation. The reason given is that the patient's energy fields are expanded and open during a spiritual operation. They take twenty-four hours to close and provide the body with protection against negative energies and attachments.

One headstrong lady from Eastern Europe insisted that she could re-enter the current rooms directly after her operation. Try as we may, we could not convince her to wait the prescribed time. The mediums of the house became very worried and kept a watchful eye over her. It wasn't long before she began to react. Within twenty minutes she began vomiting and convulsing in agony on the floor. Her open energy fields had permitted undesirable energies and attachments, shed by other sick people, to enter her body. The effects of this attack remained with her for many weeks afterwards.

Summary

- The physical body has an interactive energy counterpart referred to as the Human Energy Field (HEF), often called the *aura.*

- The HEF is the memory storehouse of all past experiences, knowledge and spiritual awareness, which enables healing mediums to sense past life trauma.

- It is the physical, emotional and spiritual protective field from which most illnesses are either defeated or accumulate to the lower density of the physical body.

- There are seven auric layers or bodies each fed by a corresponding primary chakra.

- Healing energies can be applied by direct contact with the body or through the HEF and chakras, or a combination of both.

- If a malady exits within the physical body, it will distort its counterpart in the energy matrix. Conversely, if the energy matrix is distorted it will project ill health into the body.

- Auras change with our moods. Helping the client change their attitude will encourage a healthier life force within the HEF and consequently, the physical body.

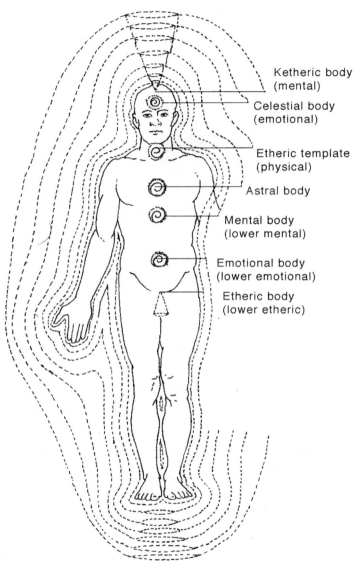

Ketheric body
(mental)

Celestial body
(emotional)

Etheric template
(physical)

Astral body

Mental body
(lower mental)

Emotional body
(lower emotional)

Etheric body
(lower etheric)

The Human Energy Field
Seven Layers with Interconnecting Primary Chakras

Fig. 6

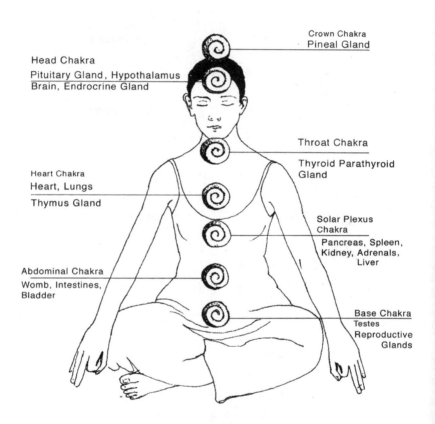

Crown Chakra
Pineal Gland

Head Chakra
Pituitary Gland, Hypothalamus
Brain, Endrocrine Gland

Throat Chakra

Thyroid Parathyroid
Gland

Heart Chakra
Heart, Lungs

Thymus Gland

Solar Plexus
Chakra

Pancreas, Spleen,
Kidney, Adrenals,
Liver

Abdominal Chakra
Womb, Intestines,
Bladder

Base Chakra
Testes
Reproductive
Glands

Glands and Organs Influenced by the Seven Primary Chakras

Fig. 7

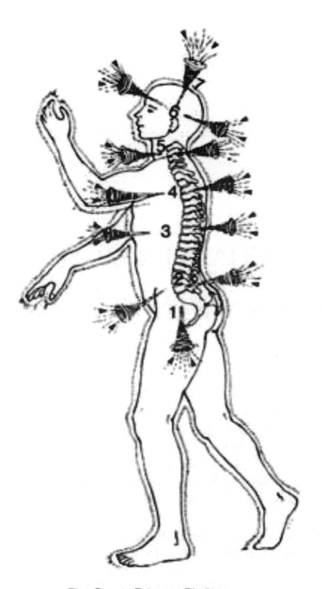

The Seven Primary Chakras

Fig. 8

CHAPTER EIGHT

MATERIALISATION OF DISEASE

"When a force in any organ or element of the body becomes deficient in its ability to reproduce that equilibrium necessary for the sustenance of physical existence and its reproduction, that portion becomes deficient in electronic energy. This may come about by injury or by disease, received by external forces. It may come from internal forces through the lack of eliminations produced in the system or by other agencies to meet its requirements in the body."[30]

This advice channelled by Edgar Cayce clearly states that the body's ill health manifests itself in a deficiency in electronic energy within the body organisms due to injury or disease, received externally or internally.

Let us examine the manifestations of illness within the human body according to five major groups of influences

Materialisation from the Human Energy Field as a result of;

— stress, worry, anxiety,
— hate, jealousy, envy,
— verbal abuse,
— dead water disease, or
— attachments.

Physically inflicted by an external influence;

— accidents,
— surgery,
— physical abuse, viruses and bacteria, pollution, or radiation (electromagnetic, nuclear, microwave etc).

Lifestyle influences.

— excessive alcohol,
— smoking,
— substance abuse,
— poor or inadequate diet,
— poisoning (pharmaceuticals and toxins— ingested or breathed), and
— lack of natural light stimulation.

Mind/Soul relationship

Karmic Debt.

Materialization from the Human Energy Field

Many purists advocate that all disease begins in the HEF and materializes into the human biological organism and, whilst in the main it may be true, it requires a belief that accidents and other externally induced catalysts are experiences directed to the individual by the 'higher self' for learning. In any case, there can be little doubt that the HEF is the energy protection shield of the physical body, fighting off external and emotional influences before they have a chance to materialise into the body's physical cellular structure. The most common ailments that can affect the HEF for transmission and materialisation include; mental abuse by family or friends, excessive stress or anxiety, hate, jealousy and negative energy attack (attachments). The resultant diseases; cancer, cysts, lethargy, asthma, headaches, arthritis etc, usually respond well to spiritual healing and intelligent counselling.

Dead water disease is a term that refers to a well documented phenomenon; people who live over stagnant, slow moving 'dead water' will draw illness from the negative energies contained therein. Research conducted in England strongly supports this theory; two rows of cottages were constructed three centuries ago along either side of a roadway. One row was built over a slow moving watercourse that emptied out into the sea nearby. The other row was built on the dry side of the road. Researchers scoured records dating back 300 years and found an exceptionally high incidence of death from cancer in the families whose houses were built over the watercourse. Most of the houses were owned by succeeding generations of families over this time. The families on the other side of the road recorded virtually no death by cancer. The theory behind this phenomenon suggests that water washes the planet from the high mountains and, as it descends, it removes negative energies from the earth's surface eventually slowing to emerge into the sea—heavy and charged with harmful energies. The salt of the sea and subsequent evaporation cleanses the water for another cycle, to be returned to the Earth as rain.

NOTE: There are two coincidental points of interest here; a basin of salt water can be used in healing clinics to absorb discarded negative energies, and, a healer should use running water to discharge negative energies from their hands after each healing session, and from their body with a shower at the end of a healing day.

Spirit attachments. An often avoided and frequently ridiculed ailment that affects over 80% of humans at some time in their lives is that of *attachments.* Attachments work exclusively through the HEF and can cause physical symptoms and mental dysfunction that defy medical science. (This subject is dealt with separately in Part II).

The disease of the tongue. Of all diseases among the human race one of the most silently destructive is the range of illnesses provoked by unkind and harsh words. We are sensitive beings of love and caring and verbal abuse upsets our vibration, our equilibrium, our balance and confidence. It enters via the HEF, ears, eyes and the mind and is stored in the subconscious. It accumulates and, in time, emerges as disease; cancer, headaches, tension, nervousness and a variety of maladies that are difficult to trace to any other source. These diseases often abate when the abused is removed from the influence of the abuser.

We are emotional beings, driven by emotions—good and bad. Every incoming emotional influence is stored somewhere within the cellular structure of the mind and body. Spiritual healing triggers a powerful release of these accumulated emotions that inhibit our lives. Some treatments release such strong feelings that the client sobs uncontrollably, sometimes without really knowing why. A post-therapeutic calm and relief is frequently obvious, often leaving the client in a mood of quiet melancholy.

Physical Influences from an External Source

Illness and disability from external sources might be indirectly influenced by many of the causes in Group 1: for example, preoccupation with stress or worry might be a contributing factor to an accident, but to try to account for every possible indirect influence is not always practical. It is important though, in counselling and therapy, that these influences are taken into consideration as an underlying cause.

Long-term post medical surgery complications are all too common. Whilst there are many dedicated and conscientious medical doctors, unfortunately there are far too many who believe that removing an organ or cutting away part of the human body will cure the problem. In fact, it fails to treat the cause and often exacerbates the problem by creating an imbalance in the harmony of the total organism.

Whilst no therapist can replace a lost organ or correct botched surgery, much can be done to relieve the pain and side effects by strengthening the HEF, inducing cellular revitalization and neutralizing the trauma.

Illnesses due to pollution, radiation, viruses and bacteria usually respond well to bio-energy spiritual healing. In addition, a good practitioner will look at the client's diet and lifestyle and recommend the services of a reliable naturopath for additional herbal and/or vitamin supplementation where deficiencies are seen, or where extra intake will help improve the condition.

Lifestyle Influences

Why human beings abuse the divine body vessel they have chosen to carry them through this life experience is difficult for many people to understand. The myriad of life-style excesses, poisons and harmful habits that we, knowingly or unconsciously, inflict upon ourselves in this age is mind-boggling. To quote the old adage "ignorance is bliss" is foolhardy and detrimental to one's health. Today there is so much to be careful of that we must each exercise a personal responsibility for ourselves to continually search for the truth in advertising, life trends and "accepted procedures" of our modern lifestyle. As practitioners it is important to awaken this responsibility in all of our clients. They must be encouraged to accept responsibility for their own lives. Educate yourself and then educate others!

There are many who are ill because of excessive consumption of alcohol, cigarettes and drugs. Add in the "unseen" poisons of colourings, additives, preservatives, insecticides and pesticides that are unknowingly ingested in alarming quantities, and it is little wonder we have such a sick society. In the USA alone, industry uses more than 80,000 chemicals—a large percentage of which are harmful to humans.

The inadequacies of diet and the lack of nutritional substance in modern foods is a major factor in poor health. Consider two of the twenty-first century's most consumed foods—sugar and wheat. The average person in the USA currently consumes 158 pounds of white sugar yearly (up from 1 pound in 1962) and white flour is the predominant ingredient in the greater portion of our daily fare—bread, cakes, cereals, pizzas, pasta. Few people realise that white flour contains NOTHING! After grinding and sifting it is bleached to make it white. There is so little substance left in processed white flour that government regulations in many countries require the addition of synthetic vitamin B to fortify it!

Our dairy products are pasteurised and homogenized, our fruit is gassed to prolong its shelf life. Add to this the long list of pesticides, insecticides, colourings, preservatives, thickeners, enhancers and emulsifiers and it is not hard to come to the conclusion that our "well balanced diet" is sorely inadequate. Despite propaganda to the contrary, supplementary vitamins are essential for the greater proportion of our population. It's not surprising that an inadequate diet is the underlying cause of many of our current illnesses. Look carefully at your patient's diet and provide free handouts to educate them. Encourage them to take responsibility for their own health.

Light is Life! It would be hard to find any other single cause that is more silently disease-promoting to the human race than the lack of natural sunlight. Synthetic light, especially some types of fluorescent lighting (warm pink), lack many of the necessary frequencies, and produce the harmful short-wave end of the ultraviolet spectrum, which will kill bacteria and can be very harmful to humans. Imagine the injury to health of a large proportion of the western working world restricted to office lighting for eight hours each day! Symptoms include lethargy, anger, frustration, declining eyesight, thinning hair and even decaying teeth. A recent survey of 100 carcinoma (skin cancer) sufferers showed that the largest percentage worked in fluorescent lighting. The lowest percentages were those who worked outdoors.

Even out of doors modern man is depriving himself of ultraviolet energy, essential to his health, by the fashionable trend of wearing sunglasses encouraged by the 'UV is harmful myth'. *Ultraviolet light is possibly the single most important element in the health of all life forms on earth.* Ignorance and promotion of sunglasses for profit lead most of the western world to believe that UV is dangerous. The truth is that UV short waves are dangerous but most of it is blocked by the earth's atmosphere! Long wave UV on the other hand is not just beneficial, it is essential.

Humanity evolved in natural sunlight over the past several million years. Our eyes are the collection cells for essential light and colour. Received and distributed by 317 million receptor cells light, in its multiple colour frequencies, is distributed into the body by an incredible network of sensor pathways. Some is directed to the cerebral cortex of the brain and some to the hypothalamus, which controls the functions of the pituitary gland, and hence the entire endocrine system and the autonomic nervous system. Why would anybody want to cut off this vital life force element by wearing sunglasses except in extreme glare such as snow or sand?

An even lesser known fact is the insidious damage done by ordinary prescription glasses that block out essential long wave UV energy. Car windscreens and house window glass has the same effect, so exposure to "natural" light through a glass window is *not* beneficial. A century ago, ninety percent of the population worked outdoors. Today ninety percent work indoors in artificial lighting. It is little wonder that humanity is creating an unhealthy society.

Mind/Soul Relationship

This is a common but seldom-recognised cause of physical / mental discord resulting in ill health. Not surprisingly it is one that responds best to *spiritual healing*. In such cases the material mind overrides the aspirations of the soul to the point where the soul is suppressed and depressed. The mind is wholly preoccupied with material life and excludes any attempt by the soul, and the indwelling God consciousness, to work in harmony towards an elevated, spiritually balanced life. Ultimately total preoccupation with the excesses and indulgences of a self-gratifying lifestyle will result in discontent and ultimately, illness. This can be even more prevalent in people with elevated souls: in time these people become discontent, confused, and sometimes very sick.

Eventually they will be forced, either through revelation or sickness, to confront the question of their purpose. Are they doing what they came here to do? Are they achieving anything of lasting value? Have they learned anything of eternal value? Have they contributed to the improvement of mankind or provided assistance to those who are struggling to survive this human experience?

The radical change in these patients after a few sessions of spiritual healing is not at all surprising. They will display a calmer, more integrated countenance with a clearer focus and a sense of well being they may not have enjoyed for some time. Most express a desire to change their life toward one that fulfils a greater purpose—to make a worthwhile contribution to the family of Man.

Karmic Debt

Karma means, as a synonym of sin, the performance

*if some action for the attainment of an object of selfish
desire, which cannot fail to be hurtful to somebody
else.[31] Karman; the cause. Karma the effect.*

Karmic Debt is the soul's accumulation of selfish
wrongdoings. It is the result of the Universal Laws of Cause and
Effect—what we do against the laws in one life accumulates and
requires corresponding selfless deeds in the same or another life
to equalise the debt.

Whilst many accept the existence of the Law of Karma, few
understand its implication in this life. Space does not permit a
lengthy study of the karmic laws of cause and effect in this book;
they are entire subjects in themselves. Suffice to say that some
illnesses and handicaps defy all efforts to bring about a state of
wellness. Often these cases are the soul-chosen effects of karma.
Whilst it is very difficult to determine such cases, the clients
themselves will often suggest karma might be the cause of their
malady. Sometimes the therapist has a vision of the circumstances.
Perhaps we are prevented from knowing too much about the
circumstances because we cannot interfere with any soul's free-
will choice, which in the case of karma, is a choice made prior to
reincarnation to right the imbalance.

As karmic illnesses are a choice of the soul, of all possible
therapies, spiritual healing may achieve the best results—spiritual
healing treats the soul as well as the body.

Anecdote

It was August 1998 in Italy. The phone call at our small
apartment in Florence was a client who had successful treatments
for cancer from Caterina. Could we please go to the Dolomites
in the north of Italy to treat her friend who had Leukaemia?

Three days later we were in St Felica, a mountain town
snuggled in the alpine pine forests not far from the Swiss border.
At first we did not recognise the common cause of the afflictions

most of the town folk seemed to have—small egg-sized tumours on the leg of a nine year old girl. Three cases of Leukaemia in the one family, ovarian tumours, brain tumours—the number of cancer patients surprised us. Not all of them serious but too many for such a small community in an environmentally healthy area. What was causing them?

We made a number of trips to St Felica to treat the townsfolk without charge. They rewarded us with affection and hearty home cooked meals. Still, the answer eluded us until, by chance, I was thumbing through a book I found in a cousin's house in Torino a few weeks later. The book fell open at a page with a map that showed the fallout path from the Chernobyl atomic power plant disaster a few years before. The trail swept down the border of Germany and France and directly over the Italian Alps. As it was forced up over the Alps it shed its deadly rain and snow upon the unsuspecting folks of St Felica and other alpine towns.

Further inquiries from the local department of health at first bought a denial. Showing the map ultimately bought a reluctant affirmation. Most of the townsfolk suffered from some form of cancerous abnormality, inflicted upon them by the silence and stealth of atomic fallout 3000 miles to the north.

Summary

- Revealing the cause of a client's illness or disease is not a simple task. It begins with careful consultation— asking questions, analysing the answers, looking for the underlying causes—there is usually more than one. During the healing session, notes should be made of intuitive revelations and client feedback during their state of deep relaxation. The real causes might not be evident until a few sessions have passed. Sometimes only a few are obvious, sometimes none. One should not despair if the causes are not revealed, often the treatments just work because the body's self-healing energies respond, the client becomes well and resumes life with an enlightened attitude.

- Disease is the result of energy deficiency due to injury or disease, received externally or internally.

- Disease manifests from one of five groups of influences.

  o From distortions of the HEF.
  o Physically inflicted by external influences.
  o Lifestyle abuses.
  o Mind/soul disharmony.
  o Karmic debt.

- The disease of the tongue is a very frequent cause of illness in human beings.

PART TWO

SPIRITUAL HEALING

CHAPTER NINE

WHAT IS SPIRITUAL HEALING?

*"Spiritual Healing is the request for energies to effect
a healing change within a patient; set in motion by
the mental requisition of the healer to Spirit Guides.
Such spirit directed healing may be in the form of
Contact Healing, Absent Healing or Auric Healing."*

**"The intelligently directed healing forces emanate
from a *non-physical realm*. Through an attuned
healer such non-physical forces are transformed
into physical effects."**[32]

Divine or Spirit Healing is common to all religions and it
has been known throughout time with all peoples, civilised
and primitive. It is dependant upon, and subject to, the healing
law that says **"there must be a thought form request for help
before any healing can take place."** In religious circles it takes
the form of prayers to God, whether the god be the Christian

God or the God of any other religion, including the incarnations of the medicine man.

Man is both a physical and spiritual being. He has a physical and a spirit body and physical and spirit mind. The two minds are intimate, one with the other and both are able to register on the consciousness. The healer's physical mind receives information concerning the patient, which it passes on to the conscious mind, from whence it is conveyed to the spirit mind, where it can be received by the spirit guide, who is in attunement with the healer.

The Three Applications of Healing

In all three accepted methods of delivering healing; *contact healing, absent healing* and *auric healing,* all require an appropriately attuned healer, spirit forces to supply the energies and remedies, and a recipient.

- *Contact Healing.* The healer is the *attuned receiver* through whom the spirit healing forces are transmitted to the patient—he/she is the means whereby non-physical energy is made physical.

- *Absent Healing.* The healer is the *communicative link* between the healing intelligence and the patient. The patient's spirit-self is the receiver of corrective directives from the healing intelligence to effect a curative change

- *Auric Healing* again requires the healer to be the *attuned receiver,* directing the spirit healing energies to the patient, bringing about the desired change via the patient's Human Energy Field.

Contact Healing

Contact Healing, Therapeutic Touch, Hands-on-healing,

Laying-on-of-Hands are all the same. Contact Healing is the most commonly used method of energy healing.

Techniques vary widely, some include supplementary (often unnecessary) gestures or rituals, but the core essence of the method is the attunement of the healer and the request for help. Placing the hands upon the body of the recipient enables Spirit to utilise the healer's hands and energy fields to deliver the healing forces to specific areas as intuitively received by the healer.

Apart from dispensing curative energies for specific ailments, the hands-on-healer revitalises the organs and various systems of the recipient. For example, a healing hand placed upon the forehead supplies energy to stimulate the body's master control gland the hypothalamus that in turn activates master glands such as the pituitary gland. Thus the entire endocrine glandular system is revitalised. Hands applied to the heart will stimulate the vascular system in the same way as energy applied to major lymph collection points will stimulate the lymphatic network. In its simplest form, *all of life* is a series of interconnected cells that pass energy from one cell to another. Healing energies, passed along this cellular structure, will induce change within the cells at a molecular level—a feeling of improved wellbeing is the result.

Absent (Distant) Healing

Thought is energy. Thought communication is possible between physical and spiritual realms. These two facts are the essentials of Absent Healing—*a thought directed request, received by spirit from a healer, for energy healing forces to be provided to a patient, irrespective of time, distance or location.*

The remarkable Edgar Cayce, known throughout the world as the "sleeping prophet," could enter a sleeping trance and within minutes locate a subject, whom he had never met, with just that person's name and address. Once the spirit connection was made he would say, "*We have the body before us*" and then proceed to diagnose the problem and recommend remedies and treatment.

In over 14,000 carefully documented stenographed cases, covering 43 years, he was never wrong. Edgar Cayce died in January 1945. He was the finest example of absent healing in modern times and left behind a library of his diagnosis' and treatments, which are now housed in the Edgar Cayce Institute, Virginia Beach USA, as a legacy for all mankind. With such irrefutable proof how could anyone doubt the reality of absent healing?

Spirit healing is a thought process. The healing is set in motion by the mental request from the healer to the healing guides for help to reach a given patient.

Auric Healing

Auric healing is not very often practiced in itself but is frequently used by healers in conjunction with *contact healing*. Healing energies can be directed at the HEF of the patient from a considerable distance but is usually projected from within a one-metre distance.

The same rules that govern absent healing apply to auric healing; an attuned healer in contact with a spirit guide who will administer the healing energies through the healer to the patient. The only difference is the distance and the local presence of the patient.

In Contact and Auric Spiritual Healing, the healer is the attuned receiver through whom the energies are received for transmission to the patient. The energies produce chemical and physical change within the patient at cellular level.

The Name—Spiritual or Spiritualism?

If ever a word evoked argument and controversy it is the word *'Spiritual'*. Far too often it is linked in peoples' minds with the word *'Spiritualism'* and yet it should not.

Spiritual Healing is not *Spiritualism*. Spiritual healing is a therapy, whilst Spiritualism is a religion.

The Collins Dictionary defines the word 'spiritual' as: *"of spirit, as opposed to matter, of the soul, especially as acted upon by God; of, proceeding from God, holy, divine, inspired."*

The word 'spiritual' used in conjunction with healing, i.e. spiritual healing, is simply a descriptive adjective to denote the type of healing it is. Spiritual healing comes from God and is therefore divine healing. Furthermore, because it comes from God, who is the Father of all of us, regardless of race or religion, it follows that spiritual healing is not the prerogative of any particular religion but His great gift to all the human family.

It is a plain statement of fact that no healer heals of himself; he is simply a channel or instrument through whom spiritual energies flow when he is engaged in his work, whether contact or distant healing.

> *"If the true Spiritual Healer abandons a title of which he should justifiably be proud, then he is not only denying the source of healing, he is denying God and denying the existence of those wonderful selfless souls who are rightly God's healing ministers in spirit and to whom all credit should be given, without any reservation, for their tireless efforts through their human instruments on this earth to help all who are sick and suffering.*
>
> *Furthermore, spiritual healing helps Man to realise his spiritual nature, thus giving him the inspiration and the knowledge of his immortality and so inspire him to live rightly in God's sight. This we believe is the true purpose of spiritual healing."[33]*

The Fundamental Principles that Govern Spiritual Healing

All of creation is governed by Universal Laws. Healing is the result of the application of specific laws.

"The source of spiritual healing is God, who created the perfect laws that govern life. Sickness follows the transgression of these laws.

Every change in the universe is the result of law-governed forces. Nothing takes place by chance or without reason. Thus our bodies are subject to definite laws that control our health from birth to grave.

Spiritual healing is the result of law-governed healing forces that induce change. For any state of change to be purposefully effected, intelligent direction is needed to administer the law-governed forces to the subject."

Harry Edwards

The Law of Harmony

Universal Laws and Mental and Spiritual Laws govern all healing. No healing can take place without harmony between Spirit, healer and patient. In the case of absent healing the patient's self-spirit acts as the receiver of healing forces.

"Sir Isaac Newton revealed the Laws of Physics but there are higher mental and spiritual laws than those used on the physical plane of life. Christ knew and used them constantly. These higher mental and spiritual laws are so powerful that they can multiply, neutralise or even reverse national laws! It is when these higher laws are used by the mind of man, that they often produce results that seem miraculous on the physical plane."[34]

Anecdote

The finest living example of spiritual healing by the incorporation of spirit guides must surely be Joao Teixeira da Faria of Abadiania, Brazil.

Joao is a full trance medium, who looses consciousness and allows spirit guides, most of them doctors during their own incarnations, to utilize his body to perform astonishing surgery and healings. He is an illiterate person who cannot read or write and has no medical instruction whatsoever and yet, when he incorporates, he becomes a skilled surgeon of remarkable abilities.

Joao Teixeira has been providing healing for the sick and injured for the past 44 years without charge. He is arguably the greatest healer of the past 2000 years. No one who observes this man perform operations, without anaesthesia or asepsis, can deny the existence of a powerful healing partnership between this simple but powerful medium and his spirit doctors. He is the living proof that healing spirits can, and do, work through suitable vessels to alleviate suffering of the sick.

Summary

- *Spiritual healing* is the request for energies to effect a healing change within a patient; set in motion by the mental requisition of the healer to spirit guides.

- All healing is governed by Universal Laws.

- Healing is dependant upon the law that states "there must be a thought form request for help before any healing can take place." *Ask and ye shall receive.*

- Spiritual healing may be implemented by *contact healing, absent healing* or *auric healing.*

- In contact and auric healing, the healer is the attuned receiver through whom the energies are received for transmission to the patient. The energies produce chemical and physical change within the patient at cellular level.

- No healer heals of himself; he is simply a channel or instrument through whom spiritual energies flow when he is engaged in his work, whether contact or distant healing.

CHAPTER TEN

MULTIPLE WORLDS &
DIMENSIONS OF EXISTENCE

In seven "worlds" or globes of our planetary chain—
only one is accessible and visible to man on Earth.
The six invisible globes of our chain are both "worlds"
and "earths" as is our own, albeit invisible.[35]

The time/space reality of our human existence on earth is
only one of multiple dimensions of existence. Science is
only now beginning to explore and accept, through the laws of
quantum physics, the actuality of multiple dimensions of
existence.

According to the "father of spiritism", Allan Kardec, there
are an infinite number of worlds, inhabitable planets, spheres
and dimensions of existence upon which and in which we, as
spirits, must experience a variety of lives to achieve a wholly
developed soul, worthy of a close association with God.

Reincarnation into only one sphere is insufficient to attain a complete development, although a number of incarnations into a single reality such as earth are often experienced. *"In proportion, as a spirit becomes purified, the body with which he clothes himself also approaches more nearly to the spirit nature. The matter of which his body is composed is less dense; he no longer crawls heavily upon the ground; his bodily needs are less gross; and the various living beings in those higher worlds are no longer obliged to destroy one another in order to feed themselves. A spirit incarnated into those worlds enjoys a greater degree of freedom and possesses, in regard to objects at a distance, orders of perception of a nature unknown to us; he sees with his eyes what we only see in thought. The purification of spirits determines the moral excellence of the corporeal beings in whom they are incarnated—the animal passions become weaker, and selfishness gives place to the sentiment of fraternity.*

Thus, in worlds of higher degree than our earth, wars are unknown because no one thinks of doing harm to his fellow beings and there is no motive for hatred and discord.

The pure spirits inhabit certain worlds but they are not confined to them as men are confined to earth; they possess, in a higher degree than others, the power of instantaneous locomotion, which is equivalent to ubiquity."[36]

Existence is but a perception. We perceive reality by what we can see, touch, smell or hear. But true perception can be much broader than that—beyond the physical reality we accept from our very limited physical senses. Based on the concept of a multiple dimensional universe, composed of levels of different vibrational rates within the same space, we can open our perception to these higher levels of reality by increasing the vibratory rate of our energy fields. Each of us can perceive within a certain vibratory frequency range. As we increase our perceptual range to higher levels of vibration, more of the spiritual (non-physical) world becomes real to us. The more we are able to use this higher sense perception (HSP) the more we are able to access the spiritual realms of reality through an expansion of perceived reality.

There are infinite expanses of dimensions without restrictions of time or geographical limitations, overseen and governed by an immense system of hierarchical beings—deities of the Supreme Being—each responsible for their segment of the immense cosmic dimensions of reality.

First we must understand and accept that we are primarily spirit. We do not cease to exist at death of the physical body; rather we simply leave the vehicle that we as spirit made in order to incarnate. This belief is the cornerstone of spiritual healing. Without accepting this principle it is difficult to comprehend the idea that spirit beings, once living in the physical earth plane, can be called upon to assist across the physical/spiritual barriers of reality. A multidimensional perception is pivotal on an irrefutable belief in survival of the soul-consciousness after death of the physical body.

To mediums, psychics and the spiritually aware there is no doubt about the existence of, not just this visible physical world, but a series of parallel invisible spirit worlds, superimposed and interdependent, one upon the other. All around and through physical matter, other grades of matter exist. Now, with the acceptance of X-rays, television, microwaves, radio waves and electricity it is easier for us to accept the reality of an unseen world. We can see the electrical frequency evidenced by lightening and the images of television and radar but cannot see radio or microwave frequencies.

All matter is made of energy. As energy frequencies slow down, matter takes form. The higher the vibration (frequency) the less likely we can see it. We can only see, touch and perceive objects in our physical time/space reality because physical matter lies within the energy frequency range that our limited senses can perceive. That beings of similar consciousness to ourselves exist in a multitude of worlds and spheres, which scientists refer to as negative time/space reality, and in dimensions invisible to our perception may be difficult for many to accept but there is such a wealth of documented evidence that even the most close-minded sceptic would find it difficult to refute. Contact and access to the assistance of discarnates (spirit guides) in a dimension beyond our physical perception is the underlying principle of spiritual healing.

Anecdote

A case from our files adequately demonstrates the reality of multiple spheres of existence.

It was a warm perfect day in Florence. A new patient was due and Caterina busied herself between patients preparing lunch. Suddenly and without cause she felt sad, oppressively despondent and lonely. She was feeling the symptoms of the new client in advance of her arrival—pre-emptive symptoms. She had little time to ponder the cause, the patient arrived.

Immediately the session began there appeared to Caterina a tall slim man who called himself Albert. The client sobbed when she heard that her late husband was in there in the room. There followed a three-way conversation with Caterina acting as the relay for messages between the discarnate spirit and the woman.

These two had shared a loving relationship when Albert was alive in the flesh. He passed over five years previously but had been unable to move on because her mourning held him in a sphere of reality too close to the physical plane. He was bound to stay close to offer her comfort and consolation. Eventually he had led his wife to us to explain that she must cease her heavy despair to allow him to move into a higher plane. This we did and Albert no longer influenced her life with sadness and longing.

Summary

- There are an infinite number of worlds, inhabitable planets, spheres and dimensions of existence.

- Scientists, in their study of quantum physics, accept that there are multiple dimensions of existence invisible to our senses.

- We perceive reality by what we can see, touch, smell or hear but this limited human perception inhibits our ability to perceive other dimensions of existence, and those who inhabit them.

- We are primarily spirit in a temporary body. Release of the spirit from the dense body through death returns it once again to the ethereal worlds of no time, no space.

- To mediums, psychics and the spiritually aware there is no doubt about the existence of parallel invisible spirit worlds, superimposed and interdependent upon our visible physical world.

CHAPTER ELEVEN

SPIRIT GUIDES

"I am absolutely convinced of the fact that those who once lived on earth can and do communicate with us. It is hardly possible to convey to the inexperienced an adequate idea of the strength and cumulative force of the evidence."

Sir William Barrett, F.R.S.

From the nineteen-century until today there have been groups of prominent, respected scientists—many of them the best-known names in science—who have worked to prove that immortality is a natural phenomenon and its study is rightfully a branch of physics. Because of their prominence and respectability many have had to face intense opposition from both traditional Christian clergy and from materialist scientists who joined together to try to suppress their findings. These brilliant men included Albert Einstein, Marconi, Thomas Edison, Prof. William James, Prof. Richet, Dr. Baraduc, Sir Arthur Conan Doyle, J.J.

Thomson (who discovered the electron) and Emmanuel Swedenborg to list but a few. All of these scientists studied and observed the conclusive proof of survival of the spirit after death and our natural ability to make contact with them—they support it without hesitation.[37]

At death, we vacate the physical body that carried us throughout the lifetime of our earth experience and revert to our true form of energy consciousness. We do not loose physical form altogether but exist within a *perispirit*—a translucent gaseous envelope of vibrational energy similar in shape to our human body. This is our normal dimension of existence—the ethereal spheres of the spirit world—spheres of infinite proportions with levels of elevation incomprehensible to our human mind. Worlds of no time, no space liberation.

Accepting the reality of multiple dimensions and the existence of spirit entities within them is the basis of understanding psychic contact. The utilisation of spirit beings from ethereal dimensions to effect positive change within a human body is the fundamental explanation of spiritual healing.

The channelled description contained in Leslie Chyten's book *The Keeper of the Flame*, is perhaps one of the best descriptions of elevated spirit guides and their interaction with humanity: "*We are the silent presence dwelling in the background of the human story. We have no names, no separate identities except as needed from time to time to serve the Creator's purpose, to fulfil His plan by guiding you throughout the ages.*

We are scattered among the faces of the earth, some living in isolation, others dwelling amongst you in cities and towns and countryside. We dwell in the world, for the sake of the world, but we are not of this world. We dwell in the ocean of Being, the realm of primordial possibility, emerging into form only when stirred by the All, by the call of Creation moving towards its return journey Home.

Your planet called us to Her, and so we are here, and so we will remain until the divine possibility of Her original vision is realized through her inhabitants. Through you!

In order to serve you, we are required to live many lifetimes among you, gathering wisdom through experience. For this purpose we have lived as the poor and the wealthy, the oppressed and the oppressors, the victims and the criminals, the sick and the healthy. In this way we know all your faces, and therefore better serve your needs from a place of understanding.

We are not here to judge, condemn or punish. We are not here to coerce or convince. We enter only when called, even if the call is a whisper locked deep inside the heart. When even the smallest part of the soul cries out with true sincerity, we answer with our presence. We are here to support each journey towards wholeness, toward unity. We are here to reveal the greatest secrets of the universe to those who are receptive to the great mystery dwelling in the heart of All That Is.

Because we live in the eternal, beyond time, beyond place, we are infinitely patient. Although we inhabit bodies, our location is everywhere and nowhere.

When needed one of us walks among you, reaching out to those who are ready to loosen the shackles of delusion, ready to shed the attachments bought about by fear, ready to know and live the truth. It is the sincere calling for liberation, and nothing else that brings forth the Saviour. The Saviour brings redemption only to the heart that longs to be emptied of self-deceit, greed, hatred, and the endless, fruitless desires that claim its attention. When the heart is bowed down in true humility, when the sincere longing for truth cries out for direction, the Saviour appears as the guide who knows the way Home.[38]

Personal Guides

We all have spirit guides to help us through this earthly experience. They do not interfere unless we are in danger but rather offer advice by thought directives, inspire us, give us inner strength, and influence our decisions through our spirit mind. They can help us overcome illness and inspire us to cultivate our virtues, but we cannot expect them to change the physical aspects of our lives—that is our choice. The Laws of Cause and Effect govern the universe so choices made by our own free will under the Law of Self Determination will have a direct effect on our lives. Asking for the aid of spirit in achieving goals is acceptable providing it lies within the rules. Calling for spirit assistance to help others for healing and charity is both noble and elevating.

"*A stationary object is going nowhere, and cannot change direction.*"[38] It is foolhardy to become immobile waiting for inspirational guidance from God or our personal guides. Action is necessary to commence movement, guides may help us change direction but they cannot live our life. We must all make decisions for ourselves. They might not always be the right decisions but, both good and bad contribute to our accumulative life experience. We should not impose tasks upon guides that are beyond their power or permission to perform. No guide is omnipotent—they have their limitations as we have ours. Above all, we should avoid "guide worship." They, like us, are answerable to God and work within the same Universal Laws. They too were once incarnate and experienced physical time/space reality on this plane and others.

It cannot be overstressed that, as in the world of the living, there are also dishonest and deceitful spirits in the lower ethereal worlds, for one does not automatically become "holy" when one dies. It is important therefore to differentiate between valuable and trivial communications and make connections only with the most advanced spirits.

Healing Guides

Healing is but one vocation of spiritual undertaking. Healing guides choose the healing faculty as their specialty in order to expand and contribute to the developing knowledge of healing, passing on advanced techniques to new generations as mankind evolves. In much the way science is expanding, so too are the arts, mathematics and music—all spiritual faculties are under constant improvement—handing down new developments and techniques to mankind as and when required for the advancement of society as a whole.

Our aura (HEF) is the mirror of our soul, our inner self, our life energy. It reflects the personality of the soul; loving, caring, kind, compassionate or bad tempered, complaining, selfish. When our thoughts are positive and elevated it is the reflected energy and finer frequencies of our aura that attracts the spirit world and draws them near. Healers are by nature compassionate and giving, so it is natural for them to attract healing spirits.

Because of its very nature, spiritual healing is divine. Its source is divine and its application utilises divine agencies—these are spirit doctors, guides and helpers. They are as varied in their specialities as they were in physical life; nurses, psychiatrists, dentists, theologians, chiropractors, surgeons and specialists. Spirit healing guides, in God's name, use their wisdom, techniques and the energy forces at their disposal to heal the sick. The part we play in the healing effort is through our faculty of attunement with those spirit doctors to whom we convey the request for help for the patient. We are the "attuned vessel" by which means the healing forces can be transmitted to the recipient.

Spirit healing guides are masters of manipulating energies, using them to overcome the causes of disease and to remove physical ill effects. These forces are of various types; *dispersal energies* for breaking up growths, dissolving unwanted formations of calcium, dissolving cataracts. *Stimulating energies* to revitalise sluggish organs, circulation, digestion and breathing thus providing qualitative energies to cells, restoring them to a revitalised healthy condition.

Spirit-directed energies come from a non-physical dimension as the precise counterparts of the physical energies but in non-physical form. The healer has neither the knowledge nor the ability to manipulate these spirit energies; he is simply the channel through whom the healing energies flow to the patient. Thus, through the healer's faculty of attunement with spirit, he is used as a transformer for the conversion of the spirit forces into their physical counterpart and is directed by the guides to the site of the healing need. The flow is normally via the healer's hands but not necessarily so; the flow can be direct to the patient. The important fact is, that *an electrochemical change is induced within the patient as a result of the attunement between the healer, spirit guide and patient following a definitive request for help.*

Healing guides very often were doctors during a physical lifetime, choosing to continue their vocation in the spirit world. Restricted by the Laws of Self Determination, they cannot interfere directly with a human choice or destiny. Their aid must be sought, usually via an attuned healer who requests the aid on behalf of the patient and then provides himself/herself as the vessel for delivery of the healing forces.

Anecdote

In Sydney, Australia, a retired criminal lawyer set out to prove that spirit and life after death did not exist. What he proved was that spirit does exist. Instead of a negative expose he wrote a supportive and intriguing book called *"A Lawyer Presents a Case for the Afterlife."* He sought and observed acclaimed mediums and healers in an effort to discredit them until finally he found himself in contact with a spirit who convinced him that they do exist. During this confrontation he defied the spirit to prove his existence. The spirit, in mental communication, told him to stand in the middle of the room. Upon doing so the spirit induced a solid push on his back that sent him flying to the floor. Unconvinced he asked the spirit to repeat it so he could brace himself. The spirit obliged and then sent him to the carpet yet again. This was repeated several times until the lawyer was finally convinced that there was a spirit behind the force.

At the healing sanctuary of Joao Teixeira in Abadiania, Brazil, photographic proof of spirit existence is frequently recorded on film, often to the surprise of the photographer. Spirits appeared on the film of one sceptical doctor who kept his disbeliefs to himself. The spirits, reading his thoughts, knew of his lack of faith and allowed themselves to appear on his film, to the utter amazement of the doctor.

Summary

- Accepting the reality of multiple dimensions and the existence of spirit entities within them is the basis of understanding psychic contact.

- Spirit guides exist. They reside in the ethereal dimensions and can be contacted for personal and healing assistance providing the request does not contravene universal laws.

- The utilisation of spirit beings from ethereal dimensions to effect positive healing results within a human body is the fundamental explanation of spiritual healing.

- A stationary object is going nowhere—guides may help us change direction but they cannot live our life. We must set goals and work towards those goals. We must make decisions for ourselves.

- Spiritual healing is divine. Its source is divine and its application utilises divine agencies. Spirit doctors, guides and helpers were once incarnate on earth.

- Spirit-directed energies come from a non-physical dimension as the precise counterparts of physical energies but in non-physical form.

- The healer is simply a channel through whom the healing energies flow to the patient.

- A molecular electrochemical change is induced within the patient as a result of the attunement between the healer, spirit guide and patient following a definitive request for help.

CHAPTER TWELVE

NO TIME, NO SPACE

*"Meditation is one way of transcending the limits of
the linear mind and allow connectedness of all things
to become an experiential reality that transcends time
and space."*[40]

E ssential to the ability of Spirit to provide healing energies
across the boundaries of ethereal/physical existence is the
concept of NO TIME, NO SPACE. Space and time are
limitations of our slow, dense physical world. They do not exist
in the ethereal dimensions. Hence distance healing and its
seemingly miraculous results cannot be evaluated by our physical
standards of comparison.

Time, according to Albert Einstein, is not linear, it is relative
and cannot exist without space, thus forming a fourth dimension
"space-time." Physicist J.S.Bell published a mathematic proof
that subatomic particles are connected in a way that transcends
time and space. This effect is immediate and does not need time

to be transmitted. Scientists now acknowledge that the ability of mediums to communicate with spirit forces is attributable to the universal interconnectedness of "all that is" in line with Bell's theory. The transcendence of time and space is essential to the understanding of distant healing, clairvoyant insights, and past life trauma.

From experiments with clairvoyants, Laurence Le Shan defines two times—*linear time* and *clairvoyant time*. In the later what occurs has sequence but no linear time frame. If the clairvoyant actively tries to interfere with the sequence of events they are thrown back into linear time and will no longer be witnessing events outside the normal here-and-now framework.[41]

To a healer time has less of a linear value than it does a causal meaning. As energy beings we store all of our experiences in the HEF. A clairvoyant healer can "see" or sense the event, accident or trauma in the patient's energy field and can transcend time to observe the event and then negate the effect by removing the energy block.

In a broader context, healing may be considered as part of an even bigger picture. We are now beginning to perceive the nature of man and the interconnectedness of all humanity, not just with each other, but also with everything else in universal creation. This subtle but powerful interconnectedness knows no boundaries of time or space. We can connect to the past, the future and other dimensions of existence. The great Edgar Cayce was able to enter a trance state and then access the records of other dimensions, utilising spirit guides to diagnose and prescribe treatments for people whom he did not know and who were at a great distance from him. In his lifetime he performed over 14,000 distant readings by circumventing the barriers of our time/space existence.

The great Brazilian healer, Joao Teixeira da Faria, is an unconscious medium who surrenders his consciousness to allow spirit guides to transcend from an ethereal dimension to this physical dimension at will, using his body as a catalyst to attract and ground themselves in the physical Earth reality. These guides incorporate into the consciousness of the medium Joao and use his body to perform remarkable medical cures. Joao has been doing this, three days a week, for the past forty-four years. That he can access other dimensions so easily and regularly is living evidence that we are capable of accessing multiple realities. Mediums and psychics know this and are only singled out as "special" because they have developed the ability to transcend time and space, and communicate with the beings who frequent those non-physical dimensions. The entities Joao Teixeira incorporates lived an earthly life many years ago, some of them in centuries past, this is only possible if the barriers of time and space are negated.

The Three Planes of Existence

It is generally accepted amongst great healers, such as Daskalos, the renowned mystic and healer of Greece, that man lives simultaneously in three planes of existence; the *gross material*, the *psychic* and the *noetic*. All three exist at different levels of vibration. Each has a specific body relative to that existence, and are linked through their etheric doubles in the HEF.

The *gross material* existence, in which we experience life in the physical body, is the lowest level and slowest vibration. It is here that we experience time and space. The material existence is often referred to as the third-dimension. There is nothing within the entire material universe that does not have a physic and noetic counterpart. Even the Earth is a living reality. No object or atom is "dead", however, the mineral, animal and plant kingdoms do not form a psychic and noetic body that can function independently of their gross material body. Animals do not have self-consciousness. Only man is an eternal entity.

The *psychic level*, or fourth dimension, is also material but has a higher level of vibration. Space is neutralised and the individual can transcend vast distances momentarily. This is the body of emotions and sentiments.

The *noetic* plane of existence, or fifth dimension, is one in which both time and space are transcended. The vibrations are more rarefied and the individual can move and act much more freely than within the other two dimensions. The individual self-consciousness can travel instantly across time and distance. It is the noetic body that enables us to express concrete as well as abstract thoughts. It is through this plane we are able to access knowledge and insights from the ethereal dimensions, regardless of linea time or physical distance. The noetic body can exist by itself and is the vehicle for the full expression of the soul consciousness.

At death the material and psychic bodies are abandoned and the individual, in the noetic body, continues to live within the psychic worlds in a similar manner as he did in the material world. Most people, immediately after death, do not realize the transition. [42]

Past Life Problems

Some people experience pain or illness carried over from a past life trauma. In our clinic files we find one such client who suffered from a severe pain in the upper left arm for years without successful medical diagnosis to locate the cause. During therapy he suddenly had a flash back to a time when he was a swordsman and, during a battle, had his left arm severed just below the shoulder. Once the scene was bought forward into his conscious mind the pain disappeared.

Einstein's space/time continuum states that the apparent linearity of events depends on the observer; "*We are too ready to accept lives as literal 'past lives' that have happened in the past in a physical setting like this one.*" Our past lives may be happening right now in a different space/time continuum.

Past life insights may be intuitively "seen" by the healer or they may receive the past-life scene when they hold their hands over the traumatised area, or even during an embrace of the client.

Discretion must be used as to whether the client is told of the incident—sometimes they are not ready to receive such unnerving news, especially if they were a brutal personality in a past life. Everybody wants to be a queen or a prince but the fact is most of us were commoners, thieves or scoundrels—then perhaps the memory is better left alone or treated by mentally requesting aid from the attending spirit guide.

Problems related to past life experiences nearly always relate to what the personality is dealing with in the current life. Thus, to heal this life's problems, dealing with or removing past-life memory may be beneficial in reducing the associated trauma.

If a block is felt in a particular area that carries the memory, clearing energy should be focused into the block. The client is asked to remember what caused the block. This will produce a mind vision of the event in the client or the healer might receive the image. Sometimes this produces a pain or emotional outburst as the memory is released. The healer must remain firm and connected to support the client through the release. It is not uncommon for a number of past-life memories to be "stacked" within the same area. In this case each successive memory must be removed and allowed to heal before the next layer is cleared.

There is always an emotional adjustment following these therapies and the client needs to rest as much as possible. Their energy fields are expanded and sensitive for a day or two so they must avoid stressful situations while the auric defences are weak.

In some cases the past life trauma is not one that can be removed in a single lifetime. It may be the result of a serious karmic debt that requires a settlement by the client but this may not be possible in just one life span. This form of karmic influence requires the help of a "rescue team" made up of trained mediums and experienced spiritists.

Future Insights

The clarity of mind and life-change perception that follows a healing is often augmented by visions of future scenarios "seen" by the therapist. These visions can refer to future possibilities open to the client, especially when new directions are necessary to effect a change in health and happiness. As healers are by nature mediums they are very often given insights to relay to the client. Whilst no spirit can intervene in a soul's free will, advice is sometimes necessary to avert a disaster that is not in keeping with the soul's life path. In such cases the advice given can bring about profound life changes in health and material wellbeing.

Visions of a new way of life or the possible victory over a confronting problem can inject new hope and confidence into a demoralized person. Such guidance can have an uplifting effect and will bring them back on track towards achieving their life goals. But such insights must be handled with discretion—the healer should consider carefully the implications of such revelations. Sometimes they are best left unrevealed. Insights are given on a need-to-know basis so avoid the misconception that a healer/medium is capable of giving psychic readings at every healing session. Clients should be told that messages are only given if and when they are necessary.

Anecdote

A beautiful forty-year-old woman came for therapy to discuss a heaviness that pervaded her for most of her life. During the initial therapy Caterina "saw" a child waiting to be born—a girl. The client had desired a child for many years but had long ago given up any hope of becoming pregnant. Her many consultations with medical specialists could find no reason for her inability to conceive—now she was being told that she would be pregnant within three months. To add to her scepticism, she was not in a reliable relationship.

During the second consultation Caterina "saw" that the woman had had a curse placed on her mother and herself by a jealous relative, who could not conceive herself. The curse had defeated the client's ability to conceive until that time. Caterina worked on her twice more and the spell lifted one night when the woman awoke disturbed. She stood in front of a large window looking out, as she turned to walk away it exploded for no apparent reason.

Just short of three months later the woman conceived from a new loving relationship. The child, a girl, is now four years old.

Summary

- The concept of no time, no space is essential to understanding distant healing and the use of spirit guides to effect healing in the earth plane.

- The interconnectedness of humanity with "All That Is" knows no boundaries of time or space. We can be connected to the past, the future and other dimensions of existence simultaneously.

- Man exists in three planes of reality at the same time; gross material, psychic and noetic. Only the noetic and its soul-consciousness survives death and is available to reincarnate.

- Healers can incorporate spirit guides who were incarnate hundreds, even thousands of years ago. This is only possible if the barriers of time and space are negated.

- Past-life insights may be intuitively "seen" by healers or "felt" when the affected area is touched. Clearing the memory block will result in improved health.

- Careful consideration is necessary before mentioning any messages or insights to the client. The client may not be ready to accept such knowledge.

- There is always an emotional adjustment following these therapies. The client needs to rest as much as possible.

- Healers are often given insights to relay that will bring about a radical change for the better in the client's life. Revelation of these insights must be carefully considered.

CHAPTER THIRTEEN

MEDIUMSHIP

Medium; *"A person used as a spiritual intermediary between the living and the dead"*
Collins English Dictionary

Mediumship is the ability of physical man to communicate with soul consciousness (spirit) in other, non-physical dimensions and to access the knowledge and forces of those spheres of reality.

Allan Kardec, the 19th century medium and writer stated, *"Every person who feels, in any degree whatever, the influence of spirits, is a medium. This faculty is inherent in man and consequently not an exclusive privilege. But it must be remarked that this faculty is not revealed in the same manner in all; each medium usually has a more profound aptitude for one particular facet."*

Mediumship exhibits itself in many forms; clairvoyance, clairaudience, psychographic, prophetic, healing etc. Mediums are usually stronger in one or more of these facets, specialising in clairvoyance, healing or spirit writing. There are also little known faculties such as *transfiguration* in which certain mediums can produce, from within their own body, a white gaseous vapour known as *ectoplasm* with which the spirit entity will construct a mask or full image of itself during the medium's deep trance. The manifested form is solid, has density and weight and may be touched—they are a manifested physical body. This form of mediumship is spectacular to observers but takes a great deal of the medium's physical strength and can be quite exhausting.

Materialisation is a carefully controlled procedure; the medium is seated against a black background under low red lights so that the ectoplasm can be more readily seen. The medium enters a deep trance and, whilst the participants meditate or pray to raise the ambient energy frequencies, the ectoplasm begins to extrude from their body, mostly their mouth. Spirits use the ectoplasm to form a physical body or body parts, clothing and objects. Helen Duncan, the great English medium, once manifested a female spirit who held conversation and answered questions with members of the audience for more than an hour. The spirit invited doctors to take her pulse and blood pressure to see that she was "real".

There is a real danger in this type of deep trance if the medium is suddenly interrupted by loud noise or strong light. Helen Duncan died within four days of a police raid during a deep trance state. Many say it was deliberate and that the police knew it would end her life.

The quality of contact with spirit is dependent on the quality of the spirit. As there are mischievous and misguided people so there are mischievous spirits—after all, they still carry the same character traits they had in their physical life. There are many levels of spirit elevation and the healer must be sure he is attuned to those who are dedicated to God's good works. Many spirits who work through ouija boards, tarot cards, and frivolous fortune telling are simply low-level spirits, not the elevated and dedicated spirits required for healing. Inexperienced novices who play with such psychic tools often bring harm to themselves for, having opened the portals to the lower (astral) levels of the spirit world, they unleash harmful entities that can create havoc.

The Fundamental Beliefs of Mediumship

Divine mediumship, of the quality required for healing work, requires the belief in some basic fundamentals;

- A belief in the existence of God.

- A belief in the immortality of the soul.

- Knowledge and respect for the Law of Cause & Effect (karma).

- A belief in reincarnation.

- That communication with spirit exists.

- That there exist multiple worlds, universes and dimensions.

- A belief in the moral teachings of the Christ.

Mediumship is the ability to communicate with a spirit (spirit consciousness) existing in another dimension. This can manifest itself in a variety of ways and in various degrees of proficiency.

The Major Forms of Mediumship

- *Clairvoyance—lit.* clear sensing. The ability to communicate with spirit by an inner vision. Spirit manifestations are normally "seen" with the *inner eye* rather than the *physical eye.*

- *Clairvision*—lit. clear seeing. Seeing spirit in physical form.

- *Clairaudience*—*lit.* clear hearing. Hearing spirit, either *subjectively* as an inner voice or *objectively* as an audible sound.

- *Psychographic*: writing messages under the influence or direction of spirit. Sometimes referred to as spirit writing.

- *Physical (manifestation or transfiguration)*: the ability to produce ecto-plasm and manifest objects and physical spirit forms whilst in deep trance. Spirit controls the medium.

- *Unconscious*: to lose consciousness and incorporate a spirit, who takes over the medium's body and actions.

- *Healing*: one who channels spirit for the purpose of healing—usually in a semi or full trance state (a state of attunement).

- *Prophetic*: to receive prophesies from spirit—transic and non-transic.

- *Clairsentience*—lit. clear thinking. Sometimes referred to as *intuitive mediumship*. To sense intuitively. To receive messages intuitively especially during meditation. This is the most common form of mediumship—most people have, perhaps unknowingly, experienced intuitive communication with spirit.

More than one type of mediumship may be evident in a

single medium; e.g. a healer can also be a clairvoyant, clairaudio, clairvisual and prophetic if the need arises.

All spiritual healers are mediums—but not all mediums are healers. Healing mediums normally exhibit an abundance of compassion and a genuine love for humanity. Their ability to contact spirit guides for the utilisation of healing forces is their primary talent. Healers are often found to have multiple facets of mediumship; they may be clairvoyant and clairaudient as well as prophetic. Relevant insights and messages are often delivered to healers, as and when it is necessary, for the well being of the patient. It may be a message from a deceased loved one that will ease loneliness or anxiety, or it may be a message direct from a spirit guide who sees the problem and provides the answers via the healer.

Suppressed or Ignored Mediumship

Suppressed Mediumship can have a physical effect on the mind or on the body—especially if the person is an elevated soul. With the lessons learned from each incarnation the soul evolves and matures. When a mature evolved soul reincarnates, the physical environment in which it finds itself can be a distraction from its preselected purpose. The host body can be influenced by material obsession or a life of opulent distraction—having a good time! In the passing of time, if the mind and the body don't try to achieve pre-birth goals, the soul can bring about a change in the person's status to encourage a different set of life priorities. These changes can be; financial demise, emotional unrest or physical maladies, which cause the person to look inward for answers. If these signs are ignored long enough it can bring on serious illness. These maladies can manifest in; unexplainable sores, severe headaches, mental disorders, cancer, prolonged illness and even serious accidents—anything that will slow the material mind to a contemplative state. This form of illness is common in people who seek the help of a spiritual healer—it is as if the soul has directed them to the healer knowing that the answers can be found there. Experienced spiritual healers will recognise the symptoms of this malady and advise the client to look within, to redirect their life style and habits towards more spiritually oriented goals. All souls need to keep in contact with "home" through prayer, mediation and reflection to achieve the lessons they desire from their current life experience.

A Word of Caution

Take care to invoke only quality spirits; just as there are good and bad people, there are also good and bad spirits. Many methods of contact open the portals for low-level astral spirits to cause havoc with deceit and bad intentions. The divine levels of knowledge from which true guidance, help and protection come are only achieved by calling on high level, dedicated spirits.

Ouija boards and uncontrolled séances are dangerous. They attract undesirable or mischievous spirits from the astral levels. Once the portals are open and the contact made it is very hard to close them off. You leave yourself open to "attachments" that literally attach themselves to your energy field. This type of "low level spirit consciousness" can then influence your thoughts and actions. They can live and satisfy the habits they enjoyed in their lifetime—alcoholism, drugs, smoking, etc.—if you share similar habits.

All contact should be through divine connection to the higher levels. **Prayer and elevated meditation provides protection. Always stay centred in the God/Christ connection.**

The healer will encounter some clients who have this type of low-level attachment, they can be mischievous and difficult because they are content where they are in the host body, and object to being encouraged to leave. This is dealt with in Chapter 15—Attachments.

Summary

- Mediumship is the ability of physical man to communicate with soul consciousness (spirit) in other, non-physical, dimensions and to access the knowledge and forces of those spheres of reality.

- Mediumship exhibits itself in many forms; clairvoyance, clairaudience, psychographic, prophetic, healing etc.

- The quality of contact with spirit is dependent on the quality of the spirit.

- Mediumship, of the quality required for healing work, requires the belief in seven basic fundamentals;

  o A belief in the existence of God.
  o A belief in the immortality of the soul.
  o Knowledge and respect for the Law of Cause & Effect (karma).
  o A belief in reincarnation.
  o That communication with spirit exists.
  o That there exist multiple worlds, universes and dimensions.
  o A belief in the moral teachings of Christ

- More than one type of mediumship may be evident in a single medium.

- Healers often display multiple forms of mediumship.

- Spiritual healers are mediums. Not all mediums are healers.

- Prayer and elevated meditation provide protection. Always stay centred in the God/Christ connection.

CHAPTER FOURTEEN

REINCARNATION & KARMA

Reincarnation

> Reincarnation; *"The belief that on the death of the body the soul (in time) transmigrates to, or is born again, in another body."*
>
> Collins Concise English Dictionary.

It is an accepted scientific fact that energy cannot simply disappear—it can only change form. As energy-beings we cannot just disappear, the energy still exists and in time can rematerialise into solid form again. This is the basis of reincarnation.

> *"For years the theory of reincarnation was a nightmare to me and I did my best to disprove it. Yet as years went by one subject after another told me the same story in spite of different and varied conscious beliefs.*

*Now, well over one thousand cases have been
investigated and I have to admit that there is such a
thing as reincarnation"[43]*

Our destiny from birth is to realise our true nature. Our
birth is like the entrance into a workshop or laboratory, where,
by work and experience, we slowly unfold our faculties. But it is
not possible to realise the divine nature in us by the experiences
of one lifetime. So we incarnate again and again. We enter into
life, we are born, we grow, we act, we finish our work and we
return. The return is called death. After a rest, during which we
grow by realising the joys we planned but did not achieve, we
return to birth again, more purified, stronger, wiser, to work
once more, so as to become more expert in thought, feeling and
action. This is the cycle known as reincarnation.[44]

Reincarnation is of particular importance to healing in that
past experiences, stored in the sub-conscious, influence our
behaviour and our attitude. Often, when a person tries to deviate
too drastically from a chosen learning path, the body will show
outward signs of rebellion; discontent, depression, and illness. A
session with a healer will normally bring the consciousness back
in line with the soul-directed aims of this life.

The principles of reincarnation are simple; we choose to be
born again into another physical life to:

—Complete previously unachieved goals,

—Make amends for past misdemeanours and indiscretions,
   or

—To undertake elevating life experiences in our pursuit of
   spiritual refinement.

Contrary to popular belief, the choice to reincarnate is not
imposed upon us—it is our own personal decision to experience

another life for soul enhancement or karmic resolution. Each time we choose to be reborn we set goals for the tasks and development we wish to achieve. The mechanisms we have to achieve this are; our accumulated experiences stored as knowledge in our consciousness, our God given free-will choice, and the help and guidance available from our fellows in the spirit dimensions.

It is unfortunate that religious dogma and restricted concepts of modern society often prevent us from developing naturally. Stepping aside from these restrictions we realize that we are forming our day-to-day existence and current life for a specific purpose, fuelled from the deep intuitive knowledge of our inner self. Living in the knowledge that we are part of a purposeful plan of self-development, which rewards us with accelerated spiritual and psychic growth.

Reincarnation is not the only way a soul can elevate—a soul may choose, as one of a multitude of choices, to work from the spirit dimension. The very spirit doctors and helpers we utilize in spiritual healing are those discarnates, who have chosen to work from that dimension.

Karma & The Law of Cause and Effect

> *"Karma is the law of spiritual dynamics that can be related to every act in daily life. 'Karma' is Sanskrit meaning "action" and implying the entire cycle of cause and effect. The law refers to accumulation of effects brought about by causes set in motion through our attitudes and actions (in this life or in previous lives)."*
> Theosophical Society

Karmic debt is a consequence of the Universal Law of Cause and Effect. Karma provides the soul with experiential opportunities for physical, mental and spiritual growth. Let us be absolutely clear on one point: karma is not inflicted upon us

by a wrathful God, it is our own choice. How absurd the idea
that disease and misery are inflicted upon us by God. Disease is
the result of cause. If you place your finger in a fire, it will be
burnt. If you go out in the cold and get soaked with rain, you
will most likely get a cold. If you allow your teeth to decay or
take no steps to overcome constipation, then your blood system
will become poisoned and you shall suffer in some way the effects.
Thus ill health is the result of the transgression of the Laws of
Health within the Laws of Cause and Effect.

Every human is constantly generating three types of force—
physical, emotional and mental. These determine not only our
mode of life now, with its successes or failures, and the state of
consciousness after death, but also our environment and
relationships with others in succeeding incarnations. The balance
of justice is not always struck within the limits of one life—that
is why reincarnation is said to be a means to an end, rather than
an end in itself. The cycles of reincarnation provide the necessary
extension of time to complete the amends in the cycle of cause
and effect.

Physical Action

If we act in such a manner as to bring happiness to others, we
will find ourselves in a fortunate environment with increased
opportunity for spreading happiness and good will. If we cause
pain to others by our action or our failure to act, we will find
ourselves in unhappy surroundings until we learn by experience a
greater wisdom in our choice of actions. The law functions not
to punish the indiscretion but to teach.

Emotional Action

The force generated on the emotional level is that of desire
and feeling. The pursuit of desire stimulates exertion and aids in
our development by binding us to the objects of desire. Thus we

may judge the wisdom of a particular desire by experiencing the results of its gratification. By experiencing the unpleasant results of unwise desires, the soul learns to raise lower desires to higher ones, ultimately to attain liberation from all desires. Through the happiness enjoyed by wise desires, the soul gains expansion and illumination.

Desire also makes opportunities. If we wish to have future opportunities in any line of endeavour, we should cultivate the present desire along that line and put that desire into action now.

Mental Action

The third force is thought. Thought is a great creative power by which one can build both habit and character—the sum total of our habits. Action is but the physical expression of thought. This is the key to power. Knowing that we become that which we think, we can deliberately set ourselves to think of those virtues and qualities that we desire to possess. Slowly the moulding power of thought builds those virtues into manifestation.

As healers we must take an elevated view of the manifestations of karma as it appears in our clients. Understanding that a soul is attempting to improve its character and position by one or more of the above choices of action, enables us to view their disease or trauma, not as a punishment, but as a brave choice this soul has made to add to its accumulated experiences towards a higher enlightenment.

Summary

- Reincarnation is based on the belief that the spirit, or soul/consciousness, survives physical death and chooses, in time, to experience physical life again.

- We choose each new physical life to complete previously unachieved goals, make amends for past indiscretions or undertake elevating experiences in our pursuit of spiritual refinement.

- Maladies caused by traumas of past-lives and stored in the subconscious memory, can be effectively relieved by Spiritual Healing.

- Karmic debt is a consequence of the Universal Law of Cause and Effect—"as ye sow, so shall ye reap."

- The law functions not to punish the indiscretion, but to teach.

- Understanding that a soul is attempting to improve its character and position, enables us to view a client's disease or trauma, not as a punishment, but as a brave choice this soul has made to add to its accumulated experiences towards a higher enlightenment.

CHAPTER FIFTEEN

ATTACHMENTS

Attachment: *The entering into the physical body of a living human by an earthbound spirit trapped in the lower astral plane. To be possessed by a discarnate spirit.*

Also referred to as *negative energy attachments, spirit attachment, possession* or *psychic attack,* an attachment is a spirit energy consciousness, complete with character, habits and personality, that "attaches" itself to the energy field of a living human in order to satisfy its emotional or habitual traits of physical existence.

A belief in survival of the soul consciousness after the death of our physical body is essential in the understanding of spirit possession. We all survive death but not all transitions are smooth, some troubled souls remain close to the physical world in the astral levels. Evolved souls reorient to their ethereal existence quickly and ascend to the higher realms of spiritual existence.

These evolved spirits never attach to a human being unless invited and then only if it is in accordance with universal laws—they may never interfere with any soul's right of self determination (free will).

All levels of reality contain spirits in abundance, those in the higher frequency levels are elevated souls who work divinely and may be called on by humans through mediumship for guidance and humanitarian work, but there are lower astral levels that are stopping-over places for souls who are so focused on material life that they must remain there until reorientation to other levels takes place—this may take many earth years. In the meantime they focus on Earth reality. Earthbound entities are simply those who did not make the natural transition to the higher planes of existence. Possession is evidence that only the physical body dies and that the soul-personality survives—we are immortal beings.

Souls held close to the physical realm—earthbound discarnates—by habits, emotions, love of physical life or disorientation need to attach to the energy field of a living person to be able sense, feel and satisfy those desires or emotions. The most prevalent example of spirit attachment in our society is the abuse of drugs and alcohol—such users almost without exception suffer from multiple spirit attachments. They exhibit characteristics outside the norm, including unsocial and violent behaviour.

That the spirit or soul of the dead may remain earthbound and influence the living is not a new concept, in fact it is as old as mankind itself. Religions of every type still cleanse their churches and prayer halls almost every day. From a modern viewpoint the practice is looked upon as a quaint symbolic ritual from bygone days but members of the clergy know it is an essential part of "cleansing" the space of discarnate spirits. From experience, and from knowledge passed down over centuries by their brethren, clergy know that burning incense and reciting prayers are the most effective means of "clearing" lost spirits. This is why most religious services contain a segment in which assistants swing incense burners into corners whilst prayers are recited. One does not have to look far to find a reference to spirit attachments in the bible:

> *"And when He had called unto him his twelve disciples, he gave them power against unclean spirits, to caste them out, and to heal all manner of sickness and all manner of disease."*[45]

Why do churches and other religious refuges have more discarnate souls that anywhere else? The answer is dependant upon the acceptance of a seldom-mentioned fact; that almost every living human being, at some time in his or her life, will be influenced by an unseen spirit. Humans, heavy with despair, sadness or anxiety invariably seek solace and help in a religious refuge where prayer and spiritual attunement causes the attachments to detach. Clergy use incense and prayer to raise the spiritual energy and God consciousness of the space, creating an environment that astral discarnates find uncomfortable.

In many societies incense and prayer are used regularly to clear undesirable spirits from private dwellings. That these astral spirits exist and should be treated with respect and concern is accepted as a normal part of life in many parts of the world. Sadly, western society shuns the idea as esoteric nonsense—much to its detriment. Asylums, hospitals and clinics of the western world are awash with unfortunates who suffer from a bewildering array of maladies both physical and mental, the greater percentages of which are experiencing the effects of spirit possession. According to respected Brazilian industrialist, pharmaceutical manufacturer and psychologist, Luis Rodrigues; *"it behoves us to improve our understanding of spirit, separating it from the superstitions involved in religious creeds, doctrines or dogmas, from rites and rituals. Likewise, do not waste time with obdurate scepticism that retards progress by postulating pseudo-scientific explanations that explain nothing."*

Knowledge and understanding of spirits, their forms of existence and their effects on physical human beings should be essential education for all, especially for those entrusted with our health and wellbeing. To use drugs or surgery to relieve, albeit unknowingly, the effects of spirit attachment is absurd. To pretend the problem doesn't exist is a slight on our imagined intellectual sophistication.

Put simply, attachments are spirit entities of a deceased person who, for a variety of reasons, want to stay close to the physical plane and continue to experience life in that dimension. The spirit of a deceased person can attach itself to the energy field of a living incarnate. This additional personality will affect the personality of the host.

US clinical psychologist, Dr Edith Fiore, believes that *"the majority of people, perhaps as many as 90%, probably suffer from some form of spirit attachment at one time or another."* Over 1500 therapists in the US alone now provide Spirit Releasement Therapy. In countries such as Brazil, China, Philippines and many European countries, the effect of spirit attachment is an acknowledged and accepted part of life.

How Does it Attach?

We are energy beings. We are protected by an energy body— a multi layered, multi coloured energy field that surrounds and permeates the physical body. While ever this protective field is strong and vibrant it will offer protection from attack from unseen forces, including the negative influence of astral spirits seeking a place of refuge to continue their enjoyment of the physical life through the body and senses of a living human. Except in the case of severe karmic reprisal, a healthy HEF and a spiritual approach to life is the best form of defence.

In most cases of *attachment* an astral soul attaches itself to the energy field of a living person when the HEF is weakened by intense emotional problems such as fear, anger, sadness or loneliness, by substance abuse or by some undesirable habit. A HEF that has been weakened by any of the aforementioned will attract an astral spirit of similar weakness—an alcoholic is more likely to attract a spirit who was also alcohol dependant during their own life in order to satisfy their craving for a drink.

A weakened HEF permits the attachment of astral energy forms (spirits) of similar frequencies to the weakened area of the HEF. Once attached, the negative spirit can influence the host's desires, thoughts and personality. Initially the host suspects or feels nothing except perhaps a "little out of sorts." There may be small changes in personality and habits, subtle at first, but stronger and more embedded as the attachment begins to assert its influence. The astral spirit "sets up home" within the host and over time, depending on the host's level of resistance and sense of wellbeing, will consolidate and strengthen its influence until the host is fully *oppressed* or *obsessed*.

The host begins to lose vibrancy and decisiveness. They may feel emotions that are out of character—unexplainable sadness, loneliness, reclusive, angry, and fearful. They may feel any of the entire range of human emotions. Add to this any form of craving that physical man can experience and one can begin to see the complexity of undesirable spirit attachment.

Some astral spirits are what is erroneously referred to as "evil" and indeed they may seem that way; they carry with them the same bitterness, hatred and spitefulness they developed in their previous lives. Often they are just plain mischievous and can wreak havoc if confronted. When they are destructive and violent they are referred to as *poltergeists*. Most astral spirits, however, are nothing more than disoriented souls so focused on physical life, without any understanding of survival after death, that they have difficulty in reorienting themselves to the spirit dimension, and seek to continue the experiences of physical life. These "lost souls" may be held earthbound by avarice, a love of money and possessions, desperate passion of a loved one left behind, jealousy or simply love of life itself.

There are those who died in horrendous circumstances—torture, fire, accident, maltreatment, murder, suicide, war or misery—and are earthbound by the shock and disbelief of the circumstances. Many who have suffered from trauma will attach to a human threatened by a similar fate in an endeavour to protect them. This is especially so in the case of traumatised children; a protective spirit, held to the physical plane by the shock of a comparable disaster, may attach to a child to ward off impending danger. The spirit then becomes an integral part of the child, often remaining with them for their entire life or until the spirit is dislodged by the strength and awareness of the host, by a controlled spirit releasement, or by the spirit's reorientation to a higher level.

Categories of Attachment

There are degrees of spirit attachment the least being no more than a diminution of the host's energy, the most being that the host's life is totally controlled by spirit. According to psychologist Louise Ireland-Frey, there are four possible degrees of spirit attachment:

- **Attachment**—when the entity is outside the host's body but staying nearby. A loose relationship.

- **Oppression**—when the entity is inside the aura of the host, affecting the host intermittently or mildly.

- **Obsession**—invasion of the physical body by the entity, who brings with it all its own personality traits and habits, including some that are far from desirable, often perplexing the host.

- **Possession**—when the invader completely pushes out the resident person's psyche and takes over the physical body through which it exhibits its own behaviours and speaks its own words.

Whatever the degree of intensity of the attachment, the spirit drains a person's mental and physical energy and impairs their life and goals, even to the point of incurring the death of the host. The attaching spirit uses the host's life force to remain on the Earth plane and in so doing manipulates the host's body and mind.

Within each of the above categories there are as many varieties and complexities as there are human lives. Each case of spirit attachment is unique, only the underlying principles remain constant.

Causes of Attachment

A basic *attachment*, or even *oppression*, as distinct from *possession* or *obsession*, is not necessarily of evil intent, it can be protective, benevolent or just lost but it is intrusive and will cause an assortment of side effects in the host body.

The underlying reason for a spirit to attach to a living host is to satisfy some form of physical desire such as:

Dependency Habit

A dependency habit developed over a lifetime such as smoking, alcohol, drugs, food or sex is one of the most common causes of attachment. A craving spirit will attach itself to a host who has a similar dependency in order to satisfy the craving still imprinted in their personality.

This is the most difficult type of spirit attachment to dislodge. Depending on the extent of the craving, the influence exerted on the host can be anything from aggravating to devastating. The worst examples appear in the spirits of fully dependent drug abusers who must still satisfy their craving after death. There are plenty of corporeal drug addicts who are open to the attachment of a drug dependant spirit. The one feeds off the other and there is no hope of dispatching the attachment unless the patient is willing to give up the habit—highly unlikely. These deeply dependant abusers are best sent for withdrawal therapy before any spirit releasement is attempted.

Love

The pain and anxiety of passing on before their partner and the inability to let go and move on, holds the spirit of the deceased close to the still incarnate partner. The host can frequently feel, sense or see the presence of the beloved. It is not uncommon for the host to take on similar mannerisms to the deceased.

This cause of attachment is all too common. The host usually feels deeply sad, melancholy and unable to enjoy life. They miss their departed partner and their sadness and loneliness holds the discarnate lover close to them and the physical world. Many such cases, once they have the cause revealed to them, show remarkable improvement in personality once the spirit departs. This is not a difficult releasement. Once the cause is revealed the patient is usually willing to let the loving spirit move in the knowledge that they will be together all too soon.

Protection

A spirit bullied or abused during their lifetime may attach to protect a defenceless host. This form of attachment is often found in children and can remain with them well into adulthood, sometimes for an entire lifetime. Because of the long period of shared life, this type is difficult to detect in a patient. It may be many sessions before the protecting spirit is revealed. Once revealed, it may take a great deal of patience to effect a departure as the guardian will not depart until they are convinced that the host is able to protect themselves. In this case both the therapist and the patient need to work together in prayer and mental requisition to encourage the spirit to leave.

Concern

Undue concern for the wellbeing of a loved one left behind will cause the spirit of the departed to attach to the bereaved in order to provide comfort or protection. Often this situation is caused by the host themselves holding the attachment in this plane by their excessive mourning. This type of attachment is not normally difficult to release. A discussion with the patient explaining that their sadness is holding the loved one to the Earth plane is often sufficient to enable them to encourage the release of the spirit from the emotional bonds that hold them.

Guilt

A soul, after death, feels deep remorse for actions it took or attitudes it adopted towards the host and will attach in an effort to find an opportunity to make amends. Unfortunately the host trudges through life weighed down with the oppression of guilt that they don't understand.

Incomplete life achievement

A particularly ambitious soul who dies an untimely death may feel cheated of its efforts to achieve certain life-goals. It may attach to a similarly ambitious host involved in comparable endeavours. Often an over zealous discarnate can lead its unwitting host in a frenzied obsession for material wealth to the detriment of the host.

Greed

An obsession with money and/or material possessions can cause the spirit, especially in the period soon after death, to attach to the beneficiary of the deceased's accumulated wealth. Inherited wealth spent frivolously often creates irrationality, unhappiness, depression and anxiety within the beneficiary due to the opposition of the attached spirit to the use of "their" money for frivolous purposes.

Karmic Revenge in Obsession and Possession

Seriously possessed persons are often the result of karmic revenge. When a major misdemeanour, such as murder, torture or deceit occurs in a previous life, the victim-spirit can be plunged into a blind rage of vengeance that knows no boundaries of time or space. Determined to extort revenge, it can take possession of the offender's reincarnated form in the physical plane and wreak havoc. Many patients in insane asylums are possessed by this type of vengeful spirit. Physically, they may have been perfectly healthy in their new life but the frequencies they created by their deceitful misdemeanours in the past life are bought with them. It is these similar base frequencies that enable the vengeful spirit to find and take over the host to inflict revenge.

This type of *obsession/possession* is not easily cleansed. The victim-spirit wants retribution and is held in the lower astral planes by his low frequencies and lack of forgiveness. The obsessed person also needs assistance to change his/her low level pulsations created by the misdemeanour, and yet, the Cosmic Laws of Atonement must be satisfied. Both need serious counselling to raise their spiritual vibrations to replace their fixations of hate, vengeance, despair, and wounded vanity with love, forgiveness, tolerance and compassion. This type of spirit releasement should only be done with the help of a spiritual *rescue group* comprised of mediums and skilled councillors who know how to effectively conduct the cleansing. The aim is to satisfy both parties whilst satisfying the Laws of Cause and Effect. This cannot be done in a single attempt but may require prolonged effort in cooperation with close family and loved ones and cooperating spiritual groups.

Symptoms of Spirit Attachment

The symptoms of spirit attachment can vary from imperceptible to violent evidenced by many signs, the most common of which are depression, irrationality, anger, irritability, timidness, unexplained sadness, indecision, and lethargy. Attachments of all types can reveal themselves in the host with signs of depression, despair, despondency, excessive joy and even in illness. The physical pain and symptoms of a departed loved one at the time of death may be felt by the remaining partner as unexplainable pain or suffering.

Symptoms associated with habit are much more obvious and often unpleasant. Drug and alcohol users are particularly obnoxious. Through the use of these substances they will develop depleted energy field protection. The attaching spirit, desperate to satisfy the craving locked in the personality memory of its consciousness, will find little resistance to locking onto the host HEF. Drug and alcohol users normally carry more than one attachment and are frequently (incorrectly) diagnosed as drug induced schizophrenics.

An attachment harbouring strong emotional ties normally manifests in sadness, depression and deep loneliness despite the fact that the host enjoys close friends and/or caring family.

An overprotective spirit can sometimes control the host body and mind to the point of domination—a frightening experience. These spirits may have been a dominating parent, possessive lover or a controlling but well-meaning relative.

Spells & Offensive Wishes

As there are good spirits and good uses of spirit, so there is bad. The casting of spells is a reality with dire consequences; illness, falling hair, dementia, sleeplessness, loss of appetite, overeating are all common symptoms found in spellbound humans. In extreme cases even death of the physical body can occur.

The ability to transmit energies and desires by thought is an accepted principle of spiritual healing, especially in absent healing, but the same method can be used to transmit damaging energies from one disgruntled human to another with effects ranging from mild to diabolic devastation.

Spiritual Healing is the most successful method of neutralising spells and negative energy attacks.

Recognising a Spirit Attachment

It is important to remember that a spirit attachment will try to impose its personality and its will upon the host, therefore any abnormal behaviour, which is not in keeping with the host's personality, is usually a significant sign. Irritability, nervousness and fidgeting are suspect. Rudeness, aggressiveness and anger signal a dominant spirit. Perhaps the most common trait is mood swings—one moment sweet and happy, the next snappy and rude as the spirit intermittently tries to take control of the host's thoughts and responses.

Recognizing spirit influence in people is not too difficult once the observer knows what symptoms to look for. There are many signs that give rise to suspicion:

1. Mood swings are prevalent but, because there are other causes of mood swings, this should not be the only symptom on which to make a judgment.

2. Unusually difficult to treat physical symptoms such as back pain, stomach ache, headaches and persistent local pain in limbs. The host may feel these because the discarnate suffered from them at death. This is often the case when the discarnate died of wounds in battle. In one clinical case the deceased was speared in the arm and died of gangrene—the host lived many years with an undiagnosable pain in the arm, which only left after spirit releasement.

3. Persistent reoccurring dreams that traumatize the host.

4. Unexplainable fear. This can be fear of flying, driving, closed spaces, heights, crowds or ridiculously simple things such as fire, sunlight, the sea, being alone or just fear of a particular location. These phobias are the result of the attached spirit having had a traumatic association with similar experiences in the past.

5. Fidgeting and uneasiness in the presence of an aware person such as a Spiritual Healer, medium or therapist. The attached spirit is uncomfortable in the presence of the healer and becomes aggravated.

6. Inability to look into the consultant's eyes, preferring to furtively glance away or around the room.

7. Split personality—agreeing one moment, denying the next.

8. Disagreeable character, argumentative and agitated.

9. Unexplainable sadness.

10. Desire to partake in uncharacteristic habits—smoking, drinking, sweet foods, and excessive sex.

In time a healer will develop an intuitive "knowing". This is a soul-to-soul recognition in which the healer's soul recognizes the additional attachment within the host. At first this may be dismissed as just imagination but with time and practice this becomes the initial recognition that alerts the observer to look for additional signs.

Spirit Releasement

The majority of clients who first present themselves for healing are carrying some kind of light, but interfering, attachment. It may be only lightly attached or moderately embedded. An experienced healer will recognise the problem during the first consultation and will proceed to encourage it to leave before dealing with the patient's physical problems. It is not necessary, in fact it may be unwise, to mention the attachment to the client as this may agitate the spirit or provoke a defensive attitude. The healer will make contact with it by thought communication once the session gets underway. **The calling for assistance from powerful and understanding spirit guides will normally result in the deviate spirit being quietly detached from the host.**

This form of minor spirit releasement rarely involves confrontation. The spirit should be approached with love and sincerity. They are humans without bodies, not monsters. Most are simply disoriented, confused, frightened or angry and in need of help, many have been earthbound for dozens if not hundreds of years without progress since their death. They need guidance and help to go to the Light.

In all forms of heavy spirit releasement it is important to counsel the host, encouraging them to seek a more spiritually aware life path. Meditation, prayer and spiritual books will raise their awareness and hence their frequency levels to avoid attracting spirits of low vibrational dimensions.

The old religious methods of exorcism by casting out demons with force is not only grossly inadequate it can be dangerous. Some embittered spirits don't take too kindly to violent eviction. Firmness, kindness, consideration and understanding achieve results remarkably quickly and even obdurate spirits eventually succumb.

It is not always necessary to tell the host that there is an attachment present—some people cannot grasp the concept and others are repugnant by the thought that their space has been invaded. In such "silent" cases there is a mental exchange between the practitioner and the host's soul consciousness, which mentally combine forces to encourage the lost discarnate to depart. In the majority of cases the attachment is only lightly affixed and will happily move on with relief at receiving some guidance and reassurance. Often, particularly if the attachment is firmly ensconced, one or more helpers are required to provide enough energetic and spiritual drive to dislodge the reluctant discarnate.

In dealing with *obsessions* or *possessions* the possessing spirits are stubbornly entrenched and may become agitated, even angry and violent.

Never be abusive or commanding to an attachment—it can provoke a dire reaction. If deeply attached, it can be violent and abusive—in such cases it is wise to have one or more assistants to aid and strengthen the therapist's energy. Only ever use quiet firmness, calling on those spirit guides with the strength and compassion to assist in dislodging and dispatching this agitated soul.

Here in the physical world, it is not only love, friendship and common interests that can bind people together; it can also be that unfoldment of consciousness we call hate. When one human being hates another they thereby release a spiritual power which, if the person towards whom the hate is directed is also hateful, binds the two together in a common "hell." This hell continues to exist as long as the persons concerned hate each other, and it can stretch over many incarnations. The parties can free themselves from their hell when they overcome their hate, but if they die with this hate in their consciousness it will inevitably haunt them on the spiritual plane because it is a spiritual reality. The one who is "dead" has, in certain cases, the possibility to pursue and "possess" his enemy if this enemy is not protected by his own thoughts, which he certainly is not if his thoughts are bitter and hateful. Had he, on the other hand overcome his hate and forgiven his enemy, this enemy would not be able to get power over him in any way at all. One must not therefore believe that one needs to be afraid of being possessed in such a way. If people with whom one has not had the best relations are dead, one should think lovingly of them, if possible pray for them that they may find peace; then one not only helps to remove one's own hell but those thought-impulses one sends to the deceased can help this enemy when he sooner or later has had enough of that "purgatory", which his hate, together with other primitive thought-climates, has created around him.

When he has prayed for help and his guardian angels have, through thought suggestion, removed the dark thoughts, every single loving impulse that is sent to him from other beings will be a helping factor and have the effect of a light in the darkness. Furthermore, when these two people meet each other in a later incarnation, that loving impulse will contribute to creating a better atmosphere between them.

The cycle of life-reincarnation-death is a complex one in which karma and revenge play a major role. Sometimes a karmic revenge can spread over a number of lifetimes until the debt is resolved or the revenger is raised to higher levels of forgiving vibrations. Deeply ensconced vengeful spirits can be very dangerous, needing the services of a rescue team. Rescue work is practiced widely in Brazil in Spiritist Centres and home spiritual circles. A group of people sit together around a table. The group is made up of one or more fully trained mediums, a few sitters, and a supervisor who acts as a counsellor for manifesting spirits. The mediums make it possible for the disturbing spirits to discuss their problems, but an important part of this work is carried out in the spirit world by higher discarnate spirits called upon for this purpose. Sometimes it is not for the healer to interfere with the cycle in the current lifetime.

In releasement of deeply ensconced spirits it is important to remember that you are treating two souls: the possessed and the possessor. Just encouraging the possessor to vacate the host is only a temporary result. To prevent the return of another spirit of similar vibrations attracted by the same low frequencies, it is important to raise the host to a higher vibrational dimension, free from the inferior influences of the lower ranges. This can be best achieved by encouraging him/her to enlarge their vibrational range by raising their spiritual and moral awareness through prayer, meditation and good counselling.

The healer will often receive mental pictures or messages revealing the cause for the spirit's possession of the host. Calm questioning of the client during therapy may confirm the insights and provide the healer with an understanding of the spirit's plight, thereby enabling the therapist to firmly but gently encourage the departure of the attached spirit.

After Effects

Post releasement symptoms range from a feeling of emptiness to exhaustion. The most common response after spirit releasement is as if a friend has been lost—a strange kind of melancholy, perhaps even loneliness. There is invariably a sense of release, a lightness of being, a feeling of happiness, and a renewed zest for life.

Rarely there may be a powerful physical effect: vomiting, diarrhoea or nausea. These symptoms will pass in a day or two.

Protecting and Clearing Self and Space

Healers must protect themselves against attachments, especially when they work with so many discontents that can harbour negative energies. The golden rule for protection is AWARENESS. Don't harbour excessive emotions; long term sadness, frustration, anger, resentment, hate, jealousy, and envy create weaknesses in the protective aura and invite the attachment of either a consoling spirit or a discarnate of similar discontent. Deal with the emotion and move on.

Mental awareness is an immediate protection response system during those times when one feels threatened. A simple thought that protection is required instantly expands and strengthens the HEF. Many people use a "white light" technique in which an imaginary white light from within is visualised expanding outwards, creating a protective field. In fact that is exactly what happens when we trigger our energy defences with an awareness thought.

Protection of self also requires the maintenance of good health both physically and mentally. Keep the aura strong and vibrating at a high frequency. Avoid excesses and habits of any kind especially mind-dulling and spirit-dampening indulgences such as alcohol and smoking. These can be enjoyed in moderation but even one heavy binge can invite an unwanted "friend". Drugs are disastrous—I have yet to see a drug user of any moderation without an attachment—unfortunately pharmaceutical dependency falls into this category too.

Do not invite possible trouble from mischievous discarnates by conducting séances or using Quija boards unless accompanied by experienced and elevated mediums. All too often, young people or inexperienced dabblers in this kind of communication invite very serious trouble from low-level discarnates, who attach to weak and susceptible humans.

Keep your life and environment happy and filled with a positive and loving attitude. Discontented spirits feed on misery and dissatisfaction. Read spiritually uplifting books such as the Allan Kadec range.

Clearing self is easiest, and most readily available, in the form of prayer. If this can take place within a church so much the better. Any classic church will do—old churches are built on powerful energy coordinates (another secret they keep to themselves), are built in energy concentrating designs and are spaces of continual spiritually divine meditation. They are a good place to meditate and clear.

Sensing Environmental Spirits

All of space is peopled by spirits. Recognizing the presence of discarnates in your environment requires a practiced sensitivity and keen observation.

1. The space has a sense of disharmony—people seem to be agitated with each other.

2. There are cold spots throughout the space especially in dark areas or corners.

3. Unexplainable noises from soft taps, creaks and rattles to slamming doors.

4. Furniture and items are moved or mysteriously disappear and reappear.

5. Unpleasant smells that defy logical source.

6. Dark shadow and movements seen by peripheral vision.

7. Appearance of full body apparitions.

8. Soft touches, caresses or a light push.

9. Animals behave erratically, often refusing to enter the space or parts of it. They growl, stare into corners or display raised hairs and discontent.

10. Often the disharmony can be sensed, especially by mediums who can see or sense the presence of discarnates.

11. Hearing voices, intuitively internal or externally physical.

    12. Undetectable and unexplainable scents or odours—
        medicinal, tobacco, colognes and even repugnant smells.

When incensing space, it is good to allow some of the incense smoke to encircle or enter your own aura. This will clean and enhance your energy fields and leave you feeling calm and tranquil. Therapists who deal with sick or troubled clients all day should cleanse their workspace and their personal fields daily.

Anecdote

In the spring of 1996 a beautiful young woman came to our Florence clinic for a first appointment. She was English, well bred, educated and from a fine middle-class family. She was in Florence to study art. After initial courtesies Caterina seemed uncharacteristically stern with her, much to my discomfort. I tried to intercede but Caterina abruptly cut me off and took the girl to the healing room. Within a few minutes she called me to help with the session. "Hold her wrists and shoulders lightly, but don't let her lash out," she said. The session of the next two hours was the most frightening spirit releasement I have ever witnessed.

This beautiful young woman was a heavy drug user. The attachments she carried were disagreeable in the least and dangerous in the extreme. As each discarnate left her body arched, her face distorted horribly and she screamed unnervingly. Three entities were encouraged to leave but those remaining lashed out violently and unleashed a string of foul language unbecoming of the woman.

We gave up short of our objective—drug users carry heavy and abusive attachments that are deeply entrenched. Unless the host is prepared to cease taking drugs there is little point in trying to effect a releasement—the discarnates know they are still attached to a host who will continue to feed their addiction.

Summary

- Spirit attachment is far more prevalent than we want to believe. Some respected opinions estimate that undesirable spirits will affect 90% of humanity at some time in their life.

- Many psychiatrists now believe that a large percentage of mentally ill people are affected by a spirit attachment.

- Variously referred to as negative energy attachments, spirit attachment, possession or psychic attack, an *attachment* is a spirit energy consciousness that "attaches" itself to the energy field of a living human.

- A common reason for a spirit to attach to a living host is to satisfy some form of earthly desire.

- *Obsession* and *possession* are often the result of karmic revenge to appease a past life transgression. These can be deeply embedded and dangerous.

- Dependency habits such as smoking, alcohol, drugs, pharmaceutical abuse, food or sex are the most common causes of serious attachment.

- An *attachment* is not necessarily of evil intent, it can be protective, benevolent or just lost, but it is intrusive and will cause uncharacteristic effects or illness in the host body.

- The most common symptoms are depression, irrationality, anger, irritability, timidness, unexplained sadness, indecision, lethargy, unexplainable aches and mood swings.

- Drug and alcohol users usually carry more than one attachment and are frequently (incorrectly) diagnosed as schizophrenic. They can be particularly obnoxious.

- There are four possible degrees of spirit attachment: attachment (light), oppression (firm), obsession (control), or possession (total control).

- Calling for assistance from powerful and elevated spirit guides will normally result in the deviate spirit being quietly detached from the host.

- In stubborn entrenched cases the attachment may become agitated, even angry. *Never be abusive or commanding to an attached spirit.* It is foolhardy and dangerous.

- Firmness, kindness, consideration and understanding, achieve results remarkably quickly and even obdurate spirits will eventually succumb.

- Healers must protect themselves against attachments, especially when they work with so many discontents. Use prayer, meditation and be of good physical and mental health. Avoid excessive substance use and unhealthy habits. Incense your living and working space regularly.

- Keep your life and environment happy and filled with a positive and loving attitude. Discontented spirits feed on misery and unhappiness.

- Treating the deeply possessed requires help—don't try it alone.

CHAPTER SIXTEEN

TAPPING THE ENERGY SOURCE

Raising Your Energy Fields

> *"This is necessary to prevent the healer from picking up negative energies or disease from the patient."*[46]
> Barbara Brennan

Your own good health is your best protection. You must take time to maintain your own wellbeing and vibrant protective energy fields by exercise, adequate rest and play, proper diet, and a high intake of vitamins and minerals, which the body uses more of when generating high energies. Always participate in life and its diversionary activities; theatre, cinema, music, sports and personal interests. Always ground yourself and come back to *this physical reality*. It is all too easy to linger in the altered states of consciousness associated with attunement. Remember, you are here to fully experience this time/space existence, so always ground yourself at the end of a day of healing sessions. Enjoy life and embrace it enthusiastically.

As an exercise to raise your energy vibrations spend some time, if not every day then every other day, in a relaxed connected state of mind. Some people may think of this as meditation but that term suggests a specific purpose, we are trying to raise our energy vibration through mental abandonment to enter a higher state of consciousness.

Sit comfortably in peaceful surroundings with soft background music. Wear comfortable clothing and sit in an upright position in a chair or on the floor. Close your eyes and begin to relax your body, calm your emotions and quiet your mind. Breath deeply into the stomach, relaxing your entire body with each breath. Spend two or three minutes relaxing and quieting your thoughts. Begin by feeling that you are reaching out to the higher realms of love and light. Feel you are floating upwards to a high spiritual space. Use whatever mind images you need to evoke that feeling; a peaceful scene of nature, a spiritual icon, or the reverence felt in a church or temple. With time you may find that one particular image takes you to this higher vibratory state quickly. Eventually this image becomes the "trigger" image to take you into the pre-attunement state prior to healing. With practice this trigger will connect you and open the energy flow quickly.

Mentally connect with your indwelling God-consciousness that joins you to all creation. Think about how microscopic we as humans are and yet our souls are the most powerful energy force in the universe. Spend a few minutes absorbing this higher vibration, expanding your thoughts outwards to the magnificence and grandeur of the cosmos. Feel the energy and wonder of all creation. Prayer and meditation will enable you to enter the altered state of consciousness necessary to receive and transmit energy— to commence the healing flow.

Healers are mediums, humans who can connect with spirit, and through connection to spirit, access the energies of healing. Healers are catalysts of energy, like a lightening rod that deliberately attracts energy to a focal point. The semi-transic state for accessing these energies is called *attunement*.

Anecdote

In the healing centre at Abadiania, Brazil, the healer Joao Teixeira has two rooms for what is called "current". These rooms have long benches on which sit many meditating mediums—as many as two hundred at times. The powerful combination of so many humans generating energy from their auric fields facilitates the healing response.

On occasions the Entity (the incorporated spirit) will call for more mediums because there is insufficient current to work with. On one occasion he asked everyone to pray as the surgery he was about to perform required "all the help he could get."

We under-estimate the power of our auric energy, but when two or more are joined together the power increases. Even the bible states: "Lord, you have promised that when two or more are gathered in your name you will grant their requests."

Summary

- Prayer and meditation will enable you to enter the altered state of consciousness necessary to receive and transmit energy—to commence the healing flow.

- Mentally connect with your indwelling God-consciousness that joins you to all creation.

- Practice quiet abandonment. Use trigger scenes or icons so that, in time, you can simply sit quietly, recall the trigger and the energy will flow.

- Your own good health is your best protection. Take time to maintain your own health and vibrant protective energy fields by proper diet, vitamins and minerals, exercise, rest and play. Always participate in life and its diversionary activities.

- Remember, you are here to fully experience this time/ space reality so always ground yourself at the end of the healing day.

CHAPTER SEVENTEEN

ATTUNEMENT

*"Development of the healing gift is the seeking of a
state of affinity or attunement between the healer and
the spirit guides or spirit doctors."*

Harry Edwards.

What is Attunement?

In spiritual healing, "attunement" is a word used specifically to
describe the subtle state between mental and spirit awareness.
It is in this altered state of consciousness that connection is made
with spirit guides. In New Age terminology it is often described
as *an adjustment of frequencies to that of the patient to effect a bio-
energy transfer*. Practitioners of other modalities might not place
too much emphasis on the part played by Spirit and God in the
healing act, nevertheless, even with these sceptics, to heal
effectively an attunement of sorts takes place and the universal
energy is channelled through the healer to the patient. Even those

who do not embrace spiritual healing, and believe they are simply tapping the universal energy source, require an altered state of mind to achieve results. The connection to spirit guides may take place, albeit unknowingly.

In either case, an altered state of consciousness is necessary—a quiet surrender to the point where the mind slows and a subtle awareness takes over—not unlike daydreaming. It is almost like dozing but with the consciousness of inner-mind awareness. In this state a subtle 'intuitive' insight occurs. During this feeling of 'attunement' or awareness, outside influences; noise, talking, problems of everyday life fade into the background and sensitivity to the client intensifies. In true spiritual healing this is where the connection to spirit guides is made and their work begins, using the healer as the physical channel to make the connection and deliver the healing energies. The term *attunement* means to attune the frequencies of the healer to those of the spirit guides.

In non-spiritual therapies there is a transfer of energies from the UEF, through the practitioner to the recipient. The altered state necessary for effective healing is not unlike the mental state referred to as *Alpha* in which the brain waves of the therapist are slowed by a practiced technique of relaxation.

Harry Edwards, the great English healer, described the state of attunement; *"We are seeking a 'mental abandonment'. Do not, however, try to make your mind blank for you will not succeed. Let the mind be gently contemplative, not unlike daydreaming where the mind drifts and thoughts wander and, as the physical mind surrenders, the spiritual mind becomes ascendant and in attunement with spirit. Think of contact with spirit and of the purpose for which the attunement is intended i.e. to heal the sick, to take away the pain and to remove causes of disease. By letting one's thoughts dwell lightly upon these associated ideas, the mind becomes amenable to intuitive thought through the spirit-self."*[47]

Although difficult to describe, attunement is so natural that there are rarely any physical symptoms by which to recognise it. You may find however that there is a tendency to shed involuntary tears—the eyes just run for no apparent reason, except perhaps as a consequence of the patient's soul relief. Uncontrollable eyelid flutter or a mild shiver up the spine as the connection is made. Very often a deep rhythmic breathing sets in or there can be an almost imperceptible body shudder accompanied by a short sharp inhalation of breath. Frequently in contact healing the practitioner might yawn profoundly, not a normal yawn but a deep sharp expellation of air from the lower lungs. This is a kind of "vacuuming" of the client's negative energies. Often the state of attunement can be more readily appreciated after returning to normal consciousness, leaving the practitioner in a state of calm tranquillity.

Method of Attunement

Sit comfortably in an upright chair in a quiet atmosphere. Be comfortable in your body and easy in your mind. Do not stress the situation or try to concentrate too hard. The light should be lowered to avoid glare and so help the eyes and mind to relax.

Quiet peaceful music also aids relaxation. Keep the purpose of the attunement as a sort of background thought so that when connection with spirit is made the purpose has not drifted from consciousness.

The first thoughts should be prayerful ones addressed to God. Try to avoid set prayers as they become mechanical and meaningless. Ask that His ministers in spirit give you guidance and that they provide the desired healing effect using you as the vessel of delivery.

Now let the mind dwell on some spiritual symbol; a flower, the wonder of the universe, the colour and majesty of a sunset or the healing image of Christ. These are only a few suggestions. The aim is to free the physical mind from the banal things of everyday life, thus giving the spirit mind the opportunity to become ascendant on the consciousness. This is the time your mental "trigger" image connects you to the healing source and to your guides. Most healers use a religious icon: Jesus, the Madonna, Buddha or a preferred saint as their healing "trigger".

After a few minutes of meditation allow the patient's problem to ascend into your thoughts. See the problem in your mind and ask that it be corrected. Keep the purpose simple, believing that a guide is listening and already commencing the treatment. Do not dwell upon the situation too long, for this may divert the mind and bring an end to attunement. Your spirit mind will be dominant and so in attunement with the Spirit. All that is necessary to commence the healing is a simple mental request for aid to the recipient.

Turning it ON

To many novices attunement and connection to spirit-delivered healing energies is imagined as a complicated and ritualistic procedure. It is not. Simply put, the technique required to "turn it on" is remarkably simple. Ultimately, each healer develops his/her own technique to commence the flow of healing energies. Healing is synonymous with faith. Faith is about belief in God, yourself and your ability to seek and receive the help of spirit entities in the ethereal dimensions. Remember this: your consciousness is connected to every other consciousness, now, past and future—you are part of the whole of creation and your potential is only limited by your belief in yourself.

—Close your eyes—this immediately slows brain activity.

—Breath deeply and slowly—rhythmic breathing relaxes the body.

—A silent prayer to God, the ultimate healing source.

—Visualise your "trigger" icon—Jesus, Madonna, Saint, Buddha etc.

—Make a silent request for the specific healing requirement.

—Deliver the healing energies by following your preferred practice or guided intuition.

Summary

- Attunement is an altered state of consciousness that permits an affinity or connection between the healer and the spirit guides or spirit doctors.

- Entering an attuned state the mind slows, and a subtle awareness takes over, not unlike daydreaming.

- Subtle physical symptoms may be noticed at the time of connection—spinal shiver, a sharp inhalation of air, a slight body shudder or involuntary tears.

- Once the connection is achieved and the healing begins hold the problem in your mind and ask that it be corrected, believing that a guide is listening and already commencing the treatment.

CHAPTER EIGHTEEN

HEALING PROCEDURES

Vibrant health is when the body energy is positive, powerful, at high speed, in good order, with no blockages.[48]

The spiritual healer, in attunement with spirit delivered energy, revitalises the client's bio-energy, removes blockages, realigns energy fields and induces healing energies at molecular level to bring about an improved state of health in the organism.

The method or technique of delivering healing energies is a matter of personal preference but in general most healers conduct the session in a simple and direct manner; following attunement to Spirit most healers begin by applying their hands on the afflicted part of the body. In cases of arthritis, tumours, injury etc. this is obvious but where there is a systemic problem such as wide spread cancer, diverse pain, asthma, viral infection etc. the energy should be delivered through the energy centres (chakras), particularly the abdominal area, the heart and the forehead. The preferred sequence for this application is also a matter of choice, although a practiced healer will be intuitively guided by Spirit.

Generally the incoming energies, especially when administered to the abdominal area, work directly upon the physical body through the endocrine system and associated organs. However, the healer should also work through those energy centres (chakras) and glands that govern the particular area of the body wherein the disease or discomfort is located. Thus energy directed into the abdominal centre (3rd charka) will affect the spleen, liver, pancreas, adrenals, kidneys, stomach and intestine. Likewise energy applied to the forehead (6th charka) will prompt the hypothalamus and pituitary to stimulate the endocrine and nervous systems. Similarly, stimulus to the heart charka will affect the vascular network and respiratory system.

Localised conditions such as arthritis and injury respond best if an application is made directly upon the afflicted area, such as the knees or hands. Systemic revitalisation through applications into the energy centres will support the local treatment.

Always carry in mind the problems of the afflicted person. Such thoughts carried in the mind of the healer are relayed to the Spirit who will respond with specific healing forces to alleviate the condition.

In The Beginning

How does a novice begin the practice of applying contact healing? An experienced healer, following attunement, will instinctively know or be guided where to begin, but for those who have not developed this "feel" or connection, it is best to have a basic routine with which to start. Commencing at one part of the body and progressively working through the three vertical zones, chakras and "sensitive" locations. In the beginning a set routine is advisable until you gain confidence. One method is to start at the feet of the prone client and apply energy to the soles of their feet, directing it up both sides of the body to clear, charge and rebalance the patient's energy fields.

After several minutes move to the side of the patient, with one hand on the sole of the patient's left foot and one on their left ankle. Then the left knee, the hip, working your way up both sides of the body joint by joint until you reach the primary chakras. Here you can chelate (draw out and recharge) the chakras two at a time—Sacral & Solar Plexus (2nd and 3rd), Heart & Throat (4th and 5th), Head (6th) and then the Crown (7th). At the 4th (Heart) charka patients often have an emotional release with tears and outbursts. When this happens compassionate counselling and encouraging the patient into deep rhythmic breathing will bring the emotion under control. At the 5th charka it is preferable to place your hand *under* the client's neck—it is more comfortable than on top. Positioning yourself at the head, you can then treat the shoulders, working your way up the neck to the temples and finally the crown charka.

A predetermined routine like this helps create confidence until the process becomes more guided and instinctive as you gain more experience. Eventually less mechanical thought will be necessary and you may feel a strong desire to deal directly with the problem areas e.g. a painful back will require direct application of energy to the spine, an erratic thyroid will call for direct attention to bring about a cellular change in the gland. Ultimately though, the whole energy field should be cleared and balanced at the end of the treatment.

Remember that there are three main forms of energy healing—contact, auric and distant—and many variations of the methods of application. The English healer Harry Edwards administered contact healing in a very direct way. Once attuned, he mentally visualised the problem and, *holding the healing purpose firmly in mind*, applied his hands directly to the problem area and sought a dispersal of the pain or problem. In contrast to most healers, Harry Edwards did not believe in aura adjustment. He was strictly a "contact healer" who sought direct relief for the problem in the true "laying on of hands" method.

New Zealand healer, Mr Colin Lambert, who has been a healer for more than thirty years, utilizes a different method; he runs his hands through the aura of a prone patient looking for the source of trauma or disharmony. This area is felt as a blockage of energy between his hands—a real physical obstruction that can be felt by almost anyone under his guidance. The removal of the blockage results in an improvement in the condition of the patient. *"Everything in the body is reflected in that energy field, so if there is a group of cells somewhere in the body, which has come out of phase with all the others, then the negative energy in that portion of the field will create a resistance to the movement of the hand above the body, and the healer will know he has reached the source of the problem in the body."[49]*

The one common factor that all healers must adhere to is to mindfully hold the thought of the problem, and mentally request dispersal of the cause:

THOUGHT IS AN ENERGY. ENERGY IS THOUGHT DIRECTED.

Without a mindful request for healing there is little result—healing is mind directed.

Ultimately you will develop your own technique—one that works for you. All energy therapists work in a variety of different ways, cultivating their personal technique during years of practical experience into one that achieves the desired results.

Altered States of Consciousness

During therapy the client will, at some time, enter a profound altered state of consciousness (ASOC), if not at the first treatment then at a later time when they have gained confidence in the healer and surrender to the therapy. They will quickly drift into a very deep sleep state. At this time their spirit will lift out of their body as the healing process proceeds. They may well experience a classic out of body experience (OBE) as they enter realms other than the earth plane, in which their body remains. Ideally, the patient should be permitted to stay in this state for as long as it takes, within reason, and allowed to return in their own time. Unfortunately the time constraints of measured appointments do not permit this unless the healer has multiple rooms from which to work.

Bringing the patient back to this reality should proceed with quiet and patience—any abrupt noise or rough handling causes the soul to jolt back into the body like a retracting rubber-band. Once you have verbal contact with them, tell them to open their eyes—this brings the mind from Alpha into Beta state. Ask them to move their feet and slowly stretch their arms. Eventually, once they have gained focus and full consciousness, have them sit up and take deep abdominal breaths until full control is regained. It is wise to have those that are profoundly affected sit in the reception area with a drink of water or warm tea until they are fully focused.

Summary

- In attunement with spirit, the healer delivers healing energies to revitalise the client's bio-energy, remove blockages, realign energy fields and induce change at molecular level to bring about an improved state of health in the organism.

- The simplest method of healing is the "laying on of hands" to the afflicted part of the body, with a mental request for healing to take place.

- Without a mindful request for healing there is little result—healing is mind directed. THOUGHT is energy. ENERGY is thought directed.

- Healing energies can be applied through the chakras and aura, or directly to the afflicted location, or a combination of both.

- Each healer develops his or her own application method.

- Patients may enter a deep trance state—an altered state of consciousness in which the soul is removed from the body alignment. Bring them back to consciousness slowly and calmly.

CHAPTER NINETEEN

SCANNING DIAGNOSTICS

The ability to diagnose psychically is an acknowledged reality, however, the use of psychic diagnosis should be used with great caution. Indiscriminate or unpractised use could result in misdiagnosis and/or unnecessary patient stress. In many countries the use of medical clairvoyants to diagnose a patient's problem is commonplace. In Sao Paolo, Brazil, there are large hospitals in which western trained medical practitioners work together with gifted sensitives on a daily basis to diagnose and treat seriously ill patients. Skilled sensitives can "see" the problem, often without touching or seeing the body. American psychic Edgar Cayce was undoubtedly the most famous in this century, correctly diagnosing and recommending treatment in over 14,000 carefully recorded cases in his lifetime. How can we doubt the effectiveness of psychic diagnosis in the face of such overwhelming evidence?

Technique

It is generally accepted that the ability to psychically diagnose is a "gift". A certain sensitivity can however be developed to a degree, with dedication and experience. Any diagnosis should always be confirmed medically with tests, scans or X-rays. Even gifted and experienced medical clairvoyants would never force an opinion without a second referral. People's lives are at stake!

Psychic diagnosis comes either as an *intuitive realisation* or as a "*visual*" *observation*.

In both cases "scanning" the body during hands-on healing produces the best results. An intuitive visualisation may come to mind revealing a growth or abnormality within the body or within a particular organ. You should always seek confirmation by comparing the observations with symptoms that could be associated with this type of malady. If you are convinced in your own mind that a problem exists, recommend the patient seek a medical test. Do not alarm the patient! Make notes of your observations in the patient's file so that you can compare them with the test results.

Scanning

When the practitioner is attuned and well into the treatment session, with hands over the suspect part of the patient's body, it is not unlikely that the hidden problem will transmit its energy-blueprint through the hands and into the energy receptors within the hands of the therapist. Hence the name 'scanning'—it is literally a sensory scanning of the body. As with psychic diagnostics this technique must be used with great caution and any problems detected treated with the same discretion.

Psychic Diagnostics

To some highly practiced "gifted" healers an image or realisation of the problem will manifest itself automatically in their mind or their clairvoyant sight. This can be either in the presence of the patient or by "remote viewing"—often occurring during sleep or deep meditation. To those so gifted, it is a way of life and happens frequently even with strangers or passers-by. Such visual or audio revelations are a normal part of their life. For the less-gifted therapist (the majority) it will require considerable practice and fastidious observation to develop the ability and to be able to utilise it in their practice.

Pre-emptive Sympathetic Symptoms

It is not uncommon for very sensitive healers to personally experience a patient's symptoms preceding the patient's arrival, especially prior to the first visit. This can be felt as deep sadness, anger, loneliness or even the symptoms of a disease such as pain in the problem area. This can be most disconcerting in early experiences but knowing why these symptoms occur eases the concern. The symptoms normally pass as the problem is released during treatment.

Anecdote

From our clinic files a case that illustrates the point is that of Dorothy. This patient had been ill for a long time but doctors could not locate the problem. I "saw" a large cyst in the left abdominal area. I recommended a medical examination and scan. The patient phoned next afternoon saying nothing was found. The image was so strong in my mind that I suggested a second opinion. Fortunately Dorothy was an old patient who trusted our judgement. The second examination revealed a cyst the size of an orange. She was scheduled for an immediate operation, and returned to robust health within a few weeks.

Summary

- Psychic diagnosis is possible for some healers but it should be used with great caution and careful consideration.

- Psychic diagnosis comes either as an intuitive realisation or as a "visual" observation. It is more easily detected during hands-on therapy.

- During hands-on scanning the problem will transmit its energy-blueprint through the hands and into the energy receptors of the healer. Thus the term "scanning".

- Some healers receive insights of the ailment intuitively or clairvoyantly. This can occur remotely without the presence of the patient.

- Healers can experience the patient's symptoms before they arrive—this is called "pre-emptive sympathetic symptoms" and will pass during the treatment.

CHAPTER TWENTY

CONSULTATION

W ithout a clear understanding of the patient's problem and its underlying causes the therapist is less likely to effectively direct the request for healing. Gaining this knowledge begins with the consultation during which the symptoms, pain, concerns, and causes of stress are revealed and noted.

Consultation can be as elaborate as a pre-printed form for the patient to fill in prior to consultation, followed by a careful discussion of the contents, or a simple informal chat during which the healer indirectly gains an insight into the underlying causes of the problems.

Some healers staunchly dismiss consultation, claiming that they will "read" the situation and tell the patient what their problem is. This is egotistical and unnecessary and they miss the opportunity to observe the client and establish a rapport. They also deny the client the opportunity to vent their problem, a therapeutic action in itself.

What is Consultation?

Consultation is a discussion in confidence between client and healer so the healer can better understand the client's problems. It is an opportunity to establish a confidential and trusting rapport between healer and client. Its success is dependent upon the degree of trust the client has in the therapist and the ability of the therapist to "read between the lines" to deduce the underlying truth. Consultation is the primary source of information, without which the therapist cannot begin to understand the real issues—issues not necessarily revealed by the client but can be felt intuitively by the healer.

To access this information the client must be made to feel at ease with the therapist and the environment of the clinic (or healing venue). Clients who seek help want to surrender—physically, emotionally and spiritually—to the therapy and the therapist. This might not happen on the first visit but it should occur by the second. To achieve this mutual trust there are some basic fundamentals to observe.

Gaining Trust & Confidence

- Be professional. Dress appropriately, not in sarongs and hippy gear. White or otherwise smart clothing presents an image of competence—even a doctor in jeans and sweatshirt, although highly skilled, does not instil much confidence.

- Be clean and well groomed—if you can't take care of yourself you will not offer much hope to your client to look after them.

- Be sincere in your concern of their problem. Be honest. If you disagree, don't argue but don't be afraid to say that you do not see it their way.

- Be warm in you responses. Let your healer's compassion exhibit the love you hold in your heart for them and all humanity in their struggle to make the most of this life.

- Talk less, listen intently.

- Maintain confidentiality of all that is revealed to you.

- Keep professional records of the consultation and update them at each new session. It is best to update these records before seeing the next client.

- Never take sides in a purported disagreement between the patient and their associates—there are always two sides to each disagreement. Don't allow the consultation become a gossip session.

- Humility is essential—NEVER MAKE OUTLANDISH CLAIMS OF SUCCESS even though you may be highly effective.

- Never make promises that you can effect a healing— God may have other plans.

- Have strength in your beliefs and in your convictions. Firmness is often necessary in dealing with difficult patients. Firmness and compassion are a difficult mix but it's an essential combination for all effective healers.

It is not always wise to allow a friend or relative to sit in on the consultation, especially the initial session. The patient might feel restricted in what they can say. Sometimes it is essential for both to be consulted but, more often than not, one person at a time is best. The friend or relative can join in after the consultation to sit quietly in meditation and provide extra current.

Time spent in consultation can assist the client to help themself. Simply discussing their problems and encouraging in them an optimistic outlook can do much to lift their spirits and help change their attitude to life. This in turn brings change to the condition of their aura (HEF) because auras change as our moods change. The mind area of the HEF is linked to the physical mind, therefore our thoughts affect the state of our aura. Encouraging kind, loving, caring and compassionate thoughts in the client creates a more vibrant and energized aura. This vibrancy is reflected back into the physical body encouraging improved health.

It must be stressed that flamboyant gestures, outlandish hocus-pocus, and extravagant claims give healing a bad name. Remain humble, listen more, talk less, be quietly professional.

To Charge or Not to Charge

The question of payment for a healing service is always one that provokes guilt and anxiety amongst healers. How can we charge for a divine gift? How can we live if we don't? Will we loose our gift or will the guides not work with us if we do? This question is a difficult one for healers. By nature they are compassionate, caring and giving people so charging for their help is always a perplexing problem.

The answer lies in the **intent**. If the primary intent is to make money, the healing energy will eventually be denied. If the intent is primarily to help others and the charge is incidental and necessary for survival, then the healing will be effective. It should always be your ambition to develop other means of income so you can give more healings free of charge, especially to those in need.

Summary

- Consultation provides an opportunity to discuss the client's problems and create a written record for future reference.

- Consultation is an opportunity for the healer to gain the client's trust and confidentiality.

- Time spent in consultation can assist the clients to help themselves. Simply discussing their problems and encouraging in them an optimistic outlook can do much to lift their spirits and help change their attitude to life

- Present a clean, calm, professional environment to set the client at ease.

- Humility is essential—NEVER MAKE OUTLANDISH CLAIMS OF SUCCESS, even though you may be highly effective.

- Never make promises that you can effect a healing— God may have other plans.

- It must be stressed that flamboyant gestures, outlandish hocus-pocus, and extravagant claims give healing a bad name. Remain humble, listen more, talk less, be quietly professional.

CHAPTER TWENTY-ONE

THE HEALING ROOM

H ealing can be performed anywhere and at any time; however, most healing therapy takes place in a pre-determined location; a room set-aside for this purpose, in a clinic or just a quiet corner at home. For frequent practice of spiritual healing it is better to have a regular location, particularly if you have strong patronage.

A healing room must be a refuge for the patient from the pressures of normal life. It must offer quietness, tranquillity and a sense of security. It should not be cluttered or unorganised, rather it should be simple and comfortable with soft adjustable lighting—preferably full spectrum light bulbs to alleviate tiredness in the healer—and gentle background music. It should be painted in light colours—white, cream or pale blue. Avoid strong colours especially red or orange—these colours are stimulating and agitating. Black is most unsuitable.

Essential furnishings include an adjustable massage table of comfortable height, well padded with a foam underlay or a couple of blankets, covered with clean fresh sheets, white or pale blue. It should be wide enough so that the patient's arms don't slip off when they descend into a deep sleep state. Use a low profile pillow with a disposable cover that can be renewed before the next client.

A small desk and three chairs; one chair for the client, one for anyone who accompanies them, and one for the therapist. A pneumatically adjustable practitioner's stool with a swivel seat, no back support, and a wheeled-base is an ideal means of being able to adjust to a comfortable position and height so that the therapist does not become fatigued. Some green plants are excellent for energy cleansing but should be kept to a minimum. The bed should be covered in a white sheet and the client should be covered with a similar cover. If the clinic is cool a light blanket may be used to keep the patient warm.

Icons and symbols, such as a cross, triangle, a picture of Christ or a small statue may be used as a focusing point and a reminder of the source of healing, but they should be kept to a minimum. A few large posters or paintings of tranquil scenes such as forests or waterfalls help induce a feeling of relaxation, but avoid a cluttered "new age" look. Light background music promotes relaxation. A compact disc player with a "repeat" function avoids untimely interruption and the need to restart after the therapy is under way.

Many healers like to prepare a bowl of heavily sea-salted water and place it out of sight in a corner, under the table or behind a plant. The negative energies released from patients are absorbed by the saline solution. It should be cleared regularly and poured into the toilet, the bowl cleansed and refilled. Coarse sea salt is the best for this purpose. Similarly a few healthy green plants drain off negative energies but the plants should be rotated weekly and permitted to recharge outdoors in natural surroundings.

Most healing rooms, like churches, need to be regularly cleared of negative energies with incense and prayer. This can be done with incense sticks or, preferably an incense burner; a small vessel in which charcoal cakes are lit and incense is burnt on the hot coals. The incenses most preferred for "clearing" are Sage, Sandalwood, Myrrh and Frankincense or special combinations of all four. Incensing is always carried out with prayers. The term "clearing" is in fact a misnomer for incense is actually used to purify and lighten the etheric density of an environment by raising the spiritual energy and God consciousness of space and the etheric body. The trinity of Frankincense, Myrrh and Sandalwood were presented at the birth of Christ—they symbolize the ultimate in spiritual consciousness and should be used frequently. In some office locations be aware of smoke detectors that might be triggered.

The practitioner should wear a white over-blouse or white shirt. Black, brown, grey or other heavy colours should be avoided. It is quite common for healers to be bare footed during sessions—there is a belief that they can maintain a connection with the earth energy for better flow of energies, but this has never been proved.

A healing room presents an opportunity to educate the public in self-care. Good clinics offer free brochures and handouts on a variety of health issues. It assists the client to seek the answers for their own continued good health and be responsible for their own and their family's well being. This kind of additional effort reflects well on the healer as a person who cares about the client's and the community's wellbeing.

Summary

- Healing can be performed anywhere and at any time; however, most therapy healing takes place in a pre-determined location—a room set-aside for this purpose, in a clinic or a quiet corner at home.

- A healing room must be a refuge from the pressures of normal life. It must offer quietness, tranquillity and a sense of security.

- It should be simple and comfortable with soft adjustable lighting and gentle background music. It should be painted in light colours—white, cream, pale blue.

- Preferred equipment includes a therapy table, white or pale blue sheets, a pillow, three chairs, a desk and an adjustable office stool.

- Therapists should avoid black or dark coloured clothing. White is preferable.

- A healing room presents an opportunity to educate the public in self-care. Provide brochures, printouts and magazines for self-education.

CHAPTER TWENTY-TWO

KNOWLEDGE
AND PRACTICAL LOGIC

"You the individual, can do more for your own health and well being than any doctor, any hospital, any drug, any exotic medical device" [50]

H umans living in our modern world are subjected to constant media marketing and inherent ignorance that distorts their understanding of fundamental health knowledge, particularly in relation to everyday products and their practicality. This especially applies to processed foods, vitamins and supplements about which the manufacturers often advertise excessive or distorted claims. Few people take the trouble to seek the truth to safeguard themselves and their families against this inaccurate data. Living instead under false beliefs that can result in ill health by miscomprehension of basic facts or just plain ignorance.

As a dedicated healer one should constantly seek the truth

through reliable research and, using simple logic to decide if it is practical and applicable. Pass this knowledge on to others so they can benefit from the knowledge. The aim is to encourage everyone to take responsibility for their own health.

Educate yourself and then educate your clients. No one is going to tell you the truth unless you seek it.

Magazine articles, scientific reports from the internet and reputable newspaper articles are all sources of information. Make multiple copies of important critiques and provide them for customers in your healing premises. The following are a few important examples:

Sunglasses

Take the example of sunglasses. Advertisements publish distorted warnings that "harmful UV rays will destroy our eyesight unless special UV filter sunglasses are worn." This is simply not true. Mankind evolved on this planet in *natural sunlight*— adapting, changing and perfecting itself in response to the natural environment of light, colour, gases (air), liquids and energies inherent on our planet.

Over millions of years our bodies have learnt to respond to the available elements to maintain good health for survival. The three main processes for maintaining a healthy body are; breathing, eating and absorption of light through the skin and the eyes. The first two are common knowledge—the importance of light via our eyes is not so well known and yet it is vital to our very existence.

Light, and especially low frequency UV wavebands, is essential to all life forms on this planet. Light is absorbed both through the skin and, more importantly, through the eyes. There are neurochemical channels from the retina to the pineal and pituitary glands, the master glands of the whole endocrine system that controls the production and release of hormones. This regulates our body chemistry and its growth, all organs of our body, including our brain, and how they function. The 300 million cell/tubes that make up our eyes absorb and then direct light and colour back into the cerebral cortex, the pituitary and pineal glands. Altogether the pituitary produces nine different hormones, some stimulate the thyroid, the adrenals, another acts on the kidneys and regulates the balance of water and salts in body fluids. Yet another affects our growth. It is responsible for the production of sex hormones, mother's nursing milk and contractions during birth. It affects our moods, our personality and our feeling of well-being.

The direct connection of the pituitary gland, via the hypothalamus to the brain and the entire nervous system is of the utmost importance in the maintenance of good health and the combating of disease. The regulating energy source for these vital functions is full spectrum natural light and colour, absorbed through the eyes.

Without regular exposure to light we would die. This is not to say we should stare at the sun but we should absorb light as often as possible in a natural way—by simply being outdoors for at least two hours every day. People in western societies spend far too much time indoors behind glass, and worse, in artificial lighting. We drive cars with tinted glass, live indoors behind windows that block out essential UV rays and work eight hours every working day in artificial lights of offices and shops. As light-beings we must ensure we have adequate exposure to natural full spectrum light. Without it we are lowering our immune systems and creating an imbalance that will result in disease. To wear sunglasses during those precious moments when we could absorb light tricks the body into thinking there is insufficient light available thereby distorting the body's natural balance. Consider this: your body produces melatonin to protect your skin during exposure to strong sunlight. Your body knows how much to produce by the amount and strength of the light it absorbs through your eyes. What do your eyes report when they are covered by sunglasses? **A less than needed amount of** melatonin. The sunglasses deliver a false reading! This is the primary cause of skin cancer, not overexposure to sunlight.

A scientific survey conducted by Dr Helen Shaw of University of Sydney's Melanoma Clinic and the London School of Hygiene & Tropical Medicine, showed that the incidence of malignant melanomas was considerably higher in office workers than in individuals who were regularly exposed to sunlight due to occupation or lifestyle. Dr Shaw found that people who worked indoors, particularly under fluorescent lights, had twice the risk of developing malignant melanomas than those who worked or regularly relaxed out of doors!

We cannot be healthy without regular exposure to natural light. We need full spectrum light, including ultra-violet, through our eyes!

- Exposure to light must be regular (at least one hour per day) but this does not necessarily mean sitting in full sunlight—it can be under cover of trees, a canopy or a hat.

- Exposure must be unhindered—NO SUNGLASSES, NO PRESCRIPTION GLASSES, NO CONTACT LENSES, NO WINDOWS (house, car or office)— just LIGHT!

- Exposure must NOT be excessive—anything in excess is harmful, even oxygen. DO NOT LOOK DIRECTLY AT THE SUN!

Maladies such as Arthritis have been shown in clinical trials to dramatically improve just by regular exposure to natural unhindered sunlight. Any activity that can be done outdoors under a tree without glasses of any kind is the simplest way to achieve results. Clinical trials by Dr Richard Liberman revealed that eyesight can be improved by up to 80% by the same method.

Microwave Exposure

The popular use of mobile phones is exposing millions of people worldwide to dangerous microwave injury. The enormous financial profits (over $200 billion a year) being made from this modern communication system ensures that the truth of this danger will be vigorously suppressed. Any scientific reports that warn users of the dangers are quickly rebutted and the telecommunication spin-doctors issue counter arguments to "bury" the research. Russian scientists, who were not subjected to the restrictions of capitalist economics, produced damming reports on the effects of microwaves on regular users of mobile phones. These reports are obtainable on the internet and should be made accessible to the general public and your clients.

The problem with mobile phones is that they are powerful transmitters of microwaves. The phone is held to the ear and harmful rays penetrate up to an inch and a half. This is not to say they should be banned but careful and restricted use is essential, especially with young children. The frequent use of mobile phones by young teenagers is dangerous. It is reprehensible to even consider that someone would allow a small child to use a cell phone. The young tissues of their brain cells are very susceptible to damage. Most individuals have no clue of the danger they are exposing themselves to by putting a microwave transmitter next to their head.

Food that is cooked or heated in microwave ovens has been radiated. That radiation is ingested when microwave food is eaten. There have been countless scientific articles written on this subject, most of which are suppressed or discredited.

Microwave ovens were originally developed by German scientists to support mobile operations during the invasion of the Soviet Union. The aim was to reduce the logistical problems associated with cooking fuels and equipment to produce edible products in far less time than traditional methods. The Russians and the Americans commandeered the technology but it was some 30 years before it was released for commercial use.

The Russians have done the most diligent research into the biological effects of microwave ovens—the results are of great concern to human health in three categories: cancer causing effects, destruction of nutritive value, and biological effects of direct exposure to microwave emissions.

The cancer link is established because:

- Heating prepared meats produces d-nitrosodiethanolamine, a well-known cancer-causing agent.

- Thawed frozen foods alter the breakdown of important sugars necessary for proper digestion.

- Cancer-causing agents are created in the protein-hydrolysate compounds in milk and cereals.

Effects on the body of microwave food:

- Unstable breakdown of microwave food alters their elemental food substances, which cause disorders in the digestive system.

- Chemical alterations in food cause malfunctions in the lymphatic system that degenerate the body's ability to protect itself against certain forms of neoplastics (cancer growths).

- Certain trace mineral formations in plant substances form cancer-causing free radicals.

- Statistically a higher percentage of cancerous growths result in the stomach and intestines.

- There is a generalized breakdown of the peripheral tissues and degeneration of the digestive and excretory functions.

In addition, microwave exposure causes significant decreases in the nutritive value of all foods.

Exposure to microwave emissions also has a negative effect upon the general biological welfare of humans including: loss of bioelectric strength, brain circuit destruction, loss of energy, hormone imbalances, nervous and lymphatic system damage, and brainwave disruptions—either from cooking apparatus or transmission stations.

Artificial Sweeteners

There is such strong scientific evidence that the long term effects of the artificial sweetener *aspartame* is devastating to the human body that it is looming as the next big class action in years to come. Here is some frightening information by scientific investigator Nancy Markle:

"When the temperature exceeds 86 degrees F, the wood alcohol in aspartame coverts to formaldehyde and then to formic acid, which in turn causes metabolic acidosis. (formic acid is the poison found in the sting of fire ants). The **methanol toxicity mimics multiple sclerosis**; thus people are being diagnosed with having multiple sclerosis in error. The multiple sclerosis is not a death sentence, where methanol toxicity is.

In the case of systemic lupus, we are finding it has become almost as rampant as multiple sclerosis, especially in 'diet' soft drink consumers. With methanol toxicity, the victims usually drink three to four 12 oz. cans per day, some even more. In the cases of systemic lupus, which is triggered by aspartame, the victim usually does not know that the aspartame is the culprit. The victim continues its use, aggravating the lupus to such a degree, that sometimes it becomes life threatening. When we get people off the aspartame, those with systemic lupus usually become asymptomatic. Unfortunately, we cannot reverse this disease.

On the other hand, in the case of those diagnosed with Multiple Sclerosis (when in reality, the disease is methanol toxicity) most of the symptoms disappear. We have seen cases where their vision has returned and even their hearing has returned. This also applies to cases of tinnitus.

If you are using aspartame (NutraSweet, Equal, Spoonful, etc.) and if you suffer from fibromyalgia symptoms, spasms, shooting pains, numbness in your legs, cramps, vertigo, dizziness, headaches, tinnitus, joint pain, depression, anxiety attacks, slurred speech, blurred vision, or memory loss—you probably have *aspartame disease!*

During a visit to a hospice, **a nurse said that six of her friends, who were heavy diet drink addicts, had all been diagnosed with MS.** This is beyond coincidence. Here is the problem. There were Congressional Hearings when aspartame was included in 100 different products. Since this initial hearing, there have been two subsequent hearings, but to no avail. Nothing has been done. The drug and chemical lobbies have very deep pockets. Now there are over 5,000 products containing this chemical, and the patent has expired! At the time of this first hearing, people were going blind. The methanol in the aspartame converts to formaldehyde in the retina of the eye. Formaldehyde is grouped in the same class of drugs as cyanide and arsenic—**DEADLY POISONS!!!** Unfortunately, it just takes longer to quietly kill, but it is killing people and causing all kinds of neurological problems.

Aspartame changes the brain's chemistry. It is the reason for severe seizures. This drug changes the dopamine level in the brain. Imagine what this drug does to patients suffering from Parkinson's Disease. This drug also causes birth defects.

There is absolutely no reason to take this product. **It is not a diet product!!** The Congressional record said, *'It makes you crave carbohydrates and will make you fat.'* Dr. Roberts stated that when he got patients off aspartame, their average weight loss was 19 pounds per person. The formaldehyde stores in the fat cells, particularly in the hips and thighs.

Aspartame is especially deadly for diabetics. All physicians know what wood alcohol will do to a diabetic. We find that physicians believe that they have patients with retinopathy, when in fact, it is caused by the aspartame. The aspartame keeps the blood sugar level out of control, causing many patients to go into a coma. Unfortunately, many have died. People were telling us at the Conference of the American College of Physicians, that they had relatives that switched from saccharin to an aspartame product and how that relative had eventually gone into a coma. Their physicians could not get the blood sugar levels under control. Thus, the patients suffered acute memory loss and eventually coma and death.

Memory loss is due to the fact that aspartic acid and phenylalanine are neurotoxic without the other amino acids found in protein. Thus it goes past the blood brain barrier and deteriorates the neurons of the brain. Dr. Russell Blaylock, neurosurgeon, said, 'The ingredients stimulate the neurons of the brain to death, causing brain damage of varying degrees.'

Women are being admitted to hospice care at 30 years of age with Alzheimer's Disease an alarmingly high percentage of these were long term diet drinkers. Dr. Blaylock and Dr. Roberts will be writing a position paper with some case histories and will post it on the Internet. According to the Conference of the American College of Physicians, '*We are talking about a plague of neurological diseases caused by this deadly poison.*'

Dr. Roberts realized what was happening when aspartame was first marketed. He said 'his diabetic patients presented memory loss, confusion, and severe vision loss.' At the Conference of the American College of Physicians, doctors admitted that they did not know. They had wondered why seizures were rampant (the phenylalanine in aspartame breaks down the seizure threshold and depletes serotonin, which causes manic depression, panic attacks, rage and violence).

I assure you that Monsanto, the creator of aspartame, knows how deadly it is. They fund the American Diabetes Association,

American Dietetic Association, Congress, and the Conference of the American College of Physicians. The New York Times, on November 15, 1996, ran an article on how the American Dietetic Association takes money from the food industry to endorse their products. Therefore, they cannot criticize any additives or tell about their link to Monsanto. How bad is this? We told a mother who had a child on NutraSweet to get off the product. The child was having grand mal seizures every day. The mother called her physician, who called the ADA, who told the doctor not to take the child off the NutraSweet. We are still trying to convince the mother that the aspartame is causing the seizures. Every time we get someone off aspartame, the seizures stop. There are 92 documented symptoms of aspartame, from coma to death. The majority of them are neurological because the aspartame destroys the nervous system.

Aspartame Disease is partially the cause to what is behind some of the mystery of the Desert Storm health problems. The burning tongue and other problems discussed in over 60 cases can be directly related to the consumption of an aspartame product. Several thousand pallets of diet drinks were shipped to the Desert Storm troops. (Remember heat can liberate the methanol from the aspartame at 86 degrees F). Diet drinks sat in the 120-degree F. Arabian sun for weeks at a time on pallets. The service men and women drank them all day long. All of their symptoms are identical to aspartame poisoning.

Dr. Roberts says 'consuming aspartame at the time of conception can cause birth defects.' According to Dr. Louis Elsas, Paediatrics Professor—Genetics, at Emory University in his testimony before Congress; 'the phenylalanine concentrates in the placenta, causing mental retardation.'

In the original lab tests, animals developed brain tumours—phenylalanine breaks down into DXP, a brain tumour agent. When they remove brain tumours, they have found high levels of aspartame in them.

Stevia, a sweet food, not an additive, that helps in the metabolism of sugar, which would be ideal for diabetics, has now been approved as a dietary supplement by the F.D.A. For years, the F.D.A. has outlawed this sweet food because of their loyalty to Monsanto.

If it says 'Sugar Free' on the label it most likely contains aspartame.

Senator Howard Hetzenbaum wrote a bill that would have warned all infants, pregnant mothers and children of the dangers of aspartame. The bill would have also instituted independent studies on the problems existing in the population—seizures, changes in brain chemistry, changes in neurological and behavioural symptoms. It was killed by the powerful drug and chemical lobbies, letting loose the hounds of disease and death on an unsuspecting public. Since the Conference of the American College of Physicians, we hope to have the help of some world leaders. **Again, please help us too. There are a lot of people out there who must be warned, please let them know this information."**

The Dangers of Soy

A raging argument about the unsuitability of soy as a nourishing food is being fought between big farming interests and a concerned scientific community. There is much to be concerned about. Soy, they argue, has been eaten by Asians for centuries but there is a difference between traditionally fermented soy (a long and slow process) and modern preparation methods. Therefore, fermented soy products such as tempeh and miso (not tofu) provide nourishment that is easily assimilated. In modern methods to produce soymilk the beans are first soaked in an alkaline solution, then heated to 115 degrees C in order to remove as much of the phytates as possible. This method also denatures the proteins so that they become difficult to digest and prevent the uptake of minerals.

The problem is *phytic acid* present in the outer layers of the bean. Also known as *phytates*, they block the uptake of essential minerals in the intestinal tract: calcium, magnesium, iron and especially zinc. This is particularly dangerous in infants as the lack of zinc jeopardizes the development of the brain and nervous system. The result is; lowered learning ability, apathy, lethargy, and mental retardation.

Scientists point to years of research that clearly prove that the isoflavones in soy products can depress thyroid function, causing goitre and autoimmune thyroid disease. In the early 1960s, goitre and hypothyroidism were reported in infants fed soybean diets. Japanese research of healthy subjects, fed only two teaspoons of soy per day for just one month, showed alarming increases in thyroid stimulating hormone (TSH), which greatly increase the risk of goitres.

Research points to an alarming co-relation between the use of infant soy formula and the rise in some serious childhood diseases. A study conducted at Cornell University Medical College showed that twice as many diabetic children had received soy formula in infancy as compared to non-diabetic children. Another study showed that the frequency of feedings with soy-based formulas in early life was significantly higher in children with autoimmune thyroid disease.

It is believed that soy based products significantly contribute to a variety of diseases:

- Death of brain cells in Alzheimer's dementia.

- Loss of perception, memory, reasoning and motor skills due to the restriction of zinc absorbsion.

- Poor development of brain and nervous system.

- Autoimmune thyroid disease.

- Goitres.

- Intestinal malfunction.

- Retarded physical maturation in boys.

- Early puberty in girls.

- Brain atrophy[51]

Why Sugar is so Toxic to the Body

In 1957, Dr William Coda Martin tried to answer the question: When is a food a food and when is it a poison? His definition of "poison" was: "Any substance applied to the body, ingested or developed within the body, which causes or may cause disease. The dictionary gives an even broader definition for "poison": *"to exert a harmful influence on, or to pervert."*

Dr Martin classified refined sugar as a poison because it has been depleted of its life forces, vitamins and minerals. "What is left consists of pure, refined carbohydrates. The body cannot utilize this refined starch and carbohydrate unless the depleted proteins, vitamins and minerals are present. Nature supplies these elements in each plant in quantities sufficient to metabolize the carbohydrate in that particular plant. Incomplete carbohydrate metabolism results in the formation of 'toxic metabolite' such as pyruvic acid and abnormal sugars containing five carbon atoms. Pyruvic acid accumulates in the brain and nervous system and the abnormal sugars in the red blood cells. These toxic metabolites interfere with the respiration of the cells. They cannot get sufficient oxygen to survive and function normally. In time, some of the cells die. This interferes with the function of a part of the body and is the beginning of degenerative disease."

Refined sugar is lethal when ingested by humans because it provides only that which nutritionists describe as "empty" or "naked" calories. It lacks the natural minerals, which are present in the sugar beet or cane. In addition, sugar is worse because it drains and leaches the body of precious vitamins and minerals through the demand its digestion, detoxification and elimination make upon one's entire system.

So essential is balance to our bodies that we have many ways to provide against the sudden shock of a heavy intake of sugar. Minerals such as sodium (from salt), potassium and magnesium (from vegetables), and calcium (from the bones) are mobilized and used in chemical transmutation; neutral acids are produced, which attempt to return the acid-alkaline balance factor of the blood to a more normal state.

Sugar taken every day produces a continuously over acid condition, and more and more minerals are required from deep in the body in the attempt to rectify the imbalance. Finally, in order to protect the blood, so much calcium is taken from the bones and teeth that decay and general weakening begin.

Excess sugar eventually affects every organ in the body. Initially, it is stored in the liver in the form of glucose (glycogen). Since the liver's capacity is limited, a daily intake of refined sugar (above the required amount of natural sugar) soon makes the liver expand like a balloon. When the liver is filled to its maximum capacity, the excess glycogen is returned to the blood in the form of fatty acids. These are taken to every part of the body and stored in the most inactive areas: the belly, the buttocks, the breasts and the thighs.

When these comparatively harmless places are completely filled, fatty acids are then distributed among active organs, such as the heart and kidneys. These begin to slow down; finally their tissues degenerate and turn to fat. The whole body is affected by their reduced ability, and abnormal blood pressure is created. The parasympathetic nervous system is affected; and organs governed by it, such as the small brain, become inactive or paralyzed. The circulatory and lymphatic systems are invaded, and the quality of the red corpuscles starts to change. An overabundance of white cells occurs, and the creation of tissue becomes slower. Our body's tolerance and immunizing power becomes more limited, so we cannot respond properly to extreme attacks, whether they be cold, heat, mosquitoes or microbes.

Excessive sugar has a strong mal-effect on the functioning of the brain. The key to orderly brain function is glutamic acid, a vital compound found in many vegetables. The B vitamins play a major role in dividing glutamic acid into antagonistic-complementary compounds, which produce a "proceed" or "control" response in the brain. B vitamins are also manufactured by symbiotic bacteria, which live in our intestines. When refined sugar is taken daily, these bacteria wither and die, and our stock of B vitamins gets very low. Too much sugar makes one sleepy; our ability to calculate and remember is lost.

Sugar: Harmful to Animals and Humans

Shipwrecked sailors who ate and drank nothing but sugar and rum for nine days surely went through some of this trauma; the tales they had to tell created a big public relations problem for the sugar pushers.

This incident occurred when a vessel carrying a cargo of sugar was shipwrecked in 1793. The five surviving sailors were finally rescued after being marooned for nine days. They were in a wasted condition due to starvation, having consumed nothing but sugar and rum.

The eminent French physiologist F. Magendie was inspired by that incident to conduct a series of experiments with animals, the results of which he published in 1816. In the experiments, he fed dogs a diet of sugar or olive oil and water. All the dogs on sugar wasted and died.

The shipwrecked sailors and the French physiologist's experimental dogs proved the same point. As a steady diet, sugar is worse than nothing. Plain water can keep you alive for quite some time. Sugar and water can kill you. Humans [and animals] are "unable to subsist on a diet of sugar."

The dead dogs in Professor Magendie's laboratory alerted

the sugar industry to the hazards of free scientific inquiry. From that day to this, the sugar industry has invested millions of dollars in behind-the-scenes, subsidized science. The best scientific names that money could buy have been hired, in the hope that they could one day come up with something at least pseudoscientific in the way of glad tidings about sugar.

It has been proved, however, that (1) sugar is a major factor in dental decay; (2) sugar in a person's diet does cause overweight; (3) removal of sugar from diets has cured symptoms of crippling, worldwide diseases such as diabetes, cancer and heart illnesses.

Sir Frederick Banting, the co discoverer of insulin, noticed in 1929 in Panama that, among sugar plantation owners who ate large amounts of their refined stuff, diabetes was common. Among native cane-cutters, who only got to chew the raw cane, he saw no diabetes.

However, the story of the public relations attempts on the part of the sugar manufacturers began in Britain in 1808 when the Committee of West India reported to the House of Commons that a prize of twenty-five guineas had been offered to anyone who could come up with the most "satisfactory" experiments to prove that unrefined sugar was good for feeding and fattening oxen, cows, hogs and sheep. Food for animals is often seasonal, always expensive. Sugar, by then, was dirt-cheap. People weren't eating it fast enough.

Naturally, the attempt to feed livestock with sugar and molasses in England in 1808 was a disaster. When the Committee on West India made its fourth report to the House of Commons, one Member of Parliament, John Curwin, reported that he had tried to feed sugar and molasses to calves without success. He suggested that perhaps someone should try again by sneaking sugar and molasses into skimmed milk. Had anything come of that, you can be sure the West Indian sugar merchants would have spread the news around the world. After this singular lack of success in pushing sugar in cow pastures, the West Indian sugar merchants gave up.

With undaunted zeal for increasing the market demand for the most important agricultural product of the West Indies, the Committee of West India was reduced to a tactic that has served the sugar pushers for almost 200 years: irrelevant and transparently silly testimonials from faraway, inaccessible people with some kind of "scientific" credentials. One early commentator called them "hired consciences."

The House of Commons committee was so hard-up for local cheerleaders on the sugar question, it was reduced to quoting a doctor from faraway Philadelphia, a leader of the recent American colonial rebellion: "The great Dr Rush of Philadelphia is reported to have said that 'sugar contains more nutrients in the same bulk than any other known substance'." (Emphasis added.) At the same time, the same Dr Rush was preaching that masturbation was the cause of insanity! If a weasel-worded statement like that was quoted, one can be sure no animal doctor could be found in Britain who would recommend sugar for the care and feeding of cows, pigs or sheep.

In the 1930s, a research dentist from Cleveland, Ohio, Dr Weston A. Price, traveled all over the world-from the lands of the Eskimos to the South Sea Islands, from Africa to New Zealand. His *Nutrition and Physical Degeneration: A Comparison of Primitive and Modern Diets and Their Effects*, which is illustrated with hundreds of photographs, was first published in 1939.

Dr Price took the whole world as his laboratory. His devastating conclusion, recorded in horrifying detail in area after area, was simple. People who live under so-called backward primitive conditions had excellent teeth and wonderful general health. They ate natural, unrefined food from their own locale. As soon as refined, sugared foods were imported as a result of contact with "civilization," physical degeneration began in a way that was definitely observable within a single generation.

Later, the sugar pushers advertised that sugar was chemically pure, topping Ivory soap in that department, being 99.9 per cent pure against Ivory's vaunted 99.44 per cent. "No food of our everyday diet is purer," we were assured.

What was meant by purity, besides the unarguable fact that all vitamins, minerals, salts, fibers and proteins had been removed in the refining process? Well, the sugar pushers came up with a new slant on purity.

"You don't have to sort it like beans, wash it like rice. Every grain is like every other. No waste attends its use. No useless bones like in meat, no grounds like coffee."

"Pure" is a favorite adjective of the sugar pushers because it means one thing to the chemists and another thing to ordinary mortals. When honey is labeled pure, this means that it is in its natural state (stolen directly from the bees who made it), with no adulteration with sucrose to stretch it and no harmful chemical residues, which may have been sprayed on the flowers. It does not mean that the honey is free from minerals like iodine, iron, calcium, phosphorus or multiple vitamins. So effective is the purification process which sugar cane and beets undergo in the refineries that sugar ends up as chemically pure as the morphine or the heroin a chemist has on the laboratory shelves. What nutritional virtue this abstract chemical purity represents, the sugar pushers never tell us.

The use of the word "carbohydrate" to describe sugar is deliberately misleading. Since the improved labeling of nutritional properties was required on packages and cans, refined carbohydrates like sugar are lumped together with those carbohydrates, which may or may not be refined. The several types of carbohydrates are added together for an overall carbohydrate total. Thus, the effect of the label is to hide the sugar content from the unwary buyer. Chemists add to the confusion by using the word "sugar" to describe an entire group of substances that are similar but not identical.

Glucose is a sugar found usually with other sugars, in fruits and vegetables. It is a key material in the metabolism of all plants and animals. Many of our principal foods are converted into glucose in our bodies. *Glucose* is always present in our bloodstream, and it is often called "blood sugar".

Dextrose, also called "corn sugar", is derived synthetically from starch. *Fructose* is fruit sugar. *Maltose* is malt sugar. *Lactose* is milk sugar. *Sucrose* is refined sugar made from sugar cane and sugar beet.

Glucose has always been an essential element in the human bloodstream. *Sucrose* addiction is something new in the history of the human animal. To use the word "sugar" to describe two substances, which are far from being identical, which have different chemical structures and which affect the body in profoundly different ways compounds confusion.

It makes possible more flimflam from the sugar pushers who tell us how important sugar is as an essential component of the human body, how it is oxidized to produce energy, how it is metabolized to produce warmth, and so on. They're talking about *glucose*, of course, which is manufactured in our bodies. However, one is led to believe that the manufacturers are talking about the *sucrose*, which is made in their refineries. When the word "sugar", meaning the glucose in your blood, might be confused with the sucrose in your Coca-Cola, it's great for the sugar pushers but it's rough on everybody else.

People have been bamboozled into thinking of their bodies the way they think of their cheque accounts. If they suspect they have low blood sugar, they are programmed to snack on vending machine candies and sodas in order to raise their blood sugar level. Actually, this is the worst thing to do. The level of glucose in their blood is apt to be low because they are addicted to sucrose. People who kick sucrose addiction and stay off sucrose find that the glucose level of their blood returns to normal and stays there.

Since the late 1960s, millions of Americans have returned to natural food. A new type of store, the natural food store, has encouraged many to become dropouts from the supermarket. Natural food can be instrumental in restoring health. Many people, therefore, have come to equate the word "natural" with "healthy." So the sugar pushers have now begun to pervert the word "natural" in order to mislead the public.

"Made from natural ingredients," the television sugar-pushers tell us about product after product. The word "from" is not accented on television. It should be. Even refined sugar is made from natural ingredients. There is nothing new about that. The natural ingredients are cane and beets. But that four-letter word "from" hardly suggests that 90 per cent of the cane and beet have been removed. Heroin, too, could be advertised as being made from natural ingredients. The opium poppy is as natural as the sugar beet. It's what man does with it that tells the story.

If you want to avoid sugar in the supermarket, there is only one sure way. Don't buy anything unless it says on the label prominently, in plain English: "No sugar added". Use of the word "carbohydrate" as a "scientific" word for sugar has become a standard defense strategy with sugar pushers and many of their medical apologists. It's their security blanket."[52]

Summary

- All of the above are readily available on the internet. All of them are vitally important to the well-being of your clients. Print off multiple copies and leave them in your healing room for your clients to take home. Attach a bold eye-catching cover sheet to prompt their curiosity.

- Be sure to read and understand the contents of the information so you can answer questions when raised.

- Have on hand a short "Recommended Reading" list of good spiritual and healing books. Most clients are inquisitive about your abilities and want to know more. Many will go on to do healing or spiritual courses for themselves. Encourage and guide them.

- Encourage your clients to take responsibility for their own health and the health of their family.

- Don't be afraid to discuss alternative options with your client. No therapist can cure every disease.

CHAPTER TWENTY-THREE

LITTLE OR NO RESPONSE

In all attempts to encourage an ill body back to wellness, there are times when it does not respond as well as we would like. There are many possible reasons for this:

- The patient fails to do their part; poor diet, smoking, substance abuse, alcohol and pharmaceutical dependency will retard the process.

- Lack of persistence. Some illnesses are deeply embedded and require repeated treatment. It takes time for real improvement to become apparent.

- Unrevealed causes. Many illnesses are caused by stress, unhappiness, past traumas, loneliness, family pressures, hereditary patterns etc. If the cause is not revealed recovery is bound to be hampered.

- The body is too weak to respond. If it has received radiation, chemotherapy, drugs, suffered excessive surgery or physical abuse, there is a point beyond which it will not respond to treatment.

- Lack of will to live. Some people have a "hidden agenda", a suppressed desire to just give up. These people often respond well to energy therapy and a logical, caring (not overindulgent) therapist. A rare few patients have such a strong blueprint for self-destruction that the best a therapist can do is to ease the trauma of passing.

- The 'Poor Me Syndrome". Some people live on a daily dose of sympathy. It is unwise to indulge them. Better results are gained if the therapist is understanding but firm.

- It may be outside the scope of the physical and spiritual laws that govern our lives.

- The cause may be psychosomatic; so firmly embedded in the patient's inner self, mind or consciousness that the therapy has little or no effect.

- Incorrect technique. A particular therapy might not work. Seek one that does. There is no single pill, herb or treatment that is a panacea for all ills! It is important for the patient to find what works best for them.

- In *energy healing*, as opposed to spiritual healing, the frequencies channelled by the healer may not match those necessary for the treatment of the client's disease. In such cases the treatment will be ineffective or marginal. *Spiritual Healing* does not rely on the frequencies or magnetism of the healer, it utilises spirit guides who have an infinite range of healing energies available to them.

A good therapist will not be so conceited as to think they have the only possible answer to every patient's ills. If your therapy is not bringing the desired results, help find a treatment that works best for the patient. Don't be afraid to say, "I think you should try another type of treatment." The patient will appreciate your honesty.

CHAPTER TWENTY-FOUR

DEATH—THE FINAL RELEASE

"Death is not a punishment, only a part of the pattern of life, a coming home, a resting place, before we continue our journey on."[53]

L ife also, is not a punishment, merely an experience, and one we all chose to have before incarnation into flesh, to expand the understanding and elevation of our soul. The suffering we endure on earth is only momentary, a blink of the eye, designed to teach and make us strong—death is the ultimate release of the spirit consciousness to return home.

In every healer's practice, in every person's life they will witness the passing of a life. Our perception of death is shrouded in misery when in fact it should be, and in many cultures is, a joyous event. The soul has completed its task and returned "home" where a splendid greeting committee is waiting to welcome them back into the primary reality. In our determination to hang onto life we ignore the obvious; our physical bodies are not meant to be infinite.

When a person is terminally ill and there is a growing need for the soul to be consoled, the spiritual healer should endeavour to bring peace to the troubled consciousness. A connection is made with Spirit in the ethereal reality and, with their aid, the person feels more at ease, less afraid. It is a preparation for returning "home". Loved ones who have passed before gather near to assist and, when the departing person is left to follow the natural course of life without interference from mind-distorting drugs, the gathering spirits are seen or sensed by both the departing and the farewelling persons. This is the great return to ethereal existence—it should be a beautiful and glorious experience. Unfortunately we live in a society that does not prepare people to die. In our hospitals, we use drugs that confuse the dying, who then enter the spirit world unconscious, unprepared and disoriented. These spirits may find themselves trapped between this world and the next in a state of confusion that can last for years. Mystical or religious fancies of being met by Christ or Buddha are misleading and confusing when the reality is that life goes on in the spirit world long after the body is turned to dust— it's just another state of reality.

The healer should take death as a natural and logical part of life. The return of the soul consciousness to pure spirit is a phenomenon of life—a heart warming realisation, especially when the body has endured pain and suffering. At the moment of passing there is no pain, only bliss, a sense of release and, having shed the burden of the dense physical body, freedom.

CONCLUSION

It is impossible to cover all aspects of spiritual healing in a single literary work. The contents of this book are purposefully concise and condensed to reveal the true basics of healing, providing answers to questions most frequently asked. The contents here are just the beginning. Use the list of reference sources in the bibliography, the study of books such as these will not only broaden and deepen your knowledge, they will increase your spiritual vibration and raise your etheric frequencies to enable easier communication to the ethereal spheres, where-in lay the help and guidance to increase your healing abilities.

The use of divine energies to heal is old as mankind. Referred to in the Bible as "the laying on of hands," it is God's natural method of healing, which has been subjugated by our own exalted sense of scientific sophistication. If "modern medicine" has only developed over the past 300-500 years, what did mankind do to heal during millions of years of human existence? He used herbs and energies supplied from a divine source. What is offered in this book is an introduction to one of humanity's oldest medical procedures. It doesn't matter if you are a medical practitioner of any category, an energy therapist, an interested observer or a parent who wants to educate themselves for the benefit of their family, *Bio-energy Spiritual Healing* can augment any healing modality, and its fundamental essence is inherent in all of us.

Being a true healer is not confined to a clinic or regular hours of work. It is a way of life. There is no clocking on and off. When you accept the divine gift of healing you take on serious responsibilities. A healing need can occur anywhere; in a store, shaking someone's hand, a brief embrace. You can change a person's life with a hug and a healing thought-request for help. The compassion to aid a fellow human being and a sincere intent is all that is needed.

The power to heal is God-given and should be respected as such. Few are empowered to help the many in need.

THE POWER TO HEAL

Advanced School
of Spiritual Healing Arts
A.S.S.H.A.
Bio-Energy Spiritual Healing
Certification Courses

Courses are now available for the study of Bio-energy Spiritual Healing. Recipients receive certification from the *Advanced School of Spiritual Healing Arts* to practice as a Spiritual Healer and the option to be ordained as a Minister of Religion.

The courses are in two parts: ASSHA 1 and ASSHA 2. Each course is concise and concentrated to give the maximum learning in just two days. Each includes practical instruction under the personal supervision of the Director of ASSHA, Robert

Pellegrino-Estrich. This course is designed to impart knowledge quickly and concisely, with real hands-on practical experience, to develop your healing abilities in an amazingly short period of time. Graduates may, after one year as a Spiritual Healer, apply for training and qualification as an ASSHA teacher, which provides them with the knowledge and direction to present their own courses, including assistance in format, promotional ideas, and personal guidance to achieve a highly reputable business in the healing arts.

You too can develop the ability to tap the resources of healing long forgotten in this modern scientific age. Learn how to use your own *Power to Heal* and become a qualified practitioner and a skilled teacher. For full details simply email, or post the application form to:

Rua Servidão Qd. 20, Lt. 05 Abadiânia – GO.
729 40–000 – Brazil
Phone: +55 62 9222-4119
E-mail: robetestrich@gmail.com
www.powertoheal.net

Please forward me, without obligation, details and costs of the next Bio-energy Spiritual Healing Certification Course.

My Name is: . . . .
Address: . . . .
Telephone: . . . . Fax No. . . . .
Email address: . . . .

Rua Servidão Qd. 20, Lt. 05 Abadiânia – GO.
729 40–000 – Brazil
Phone: +55 62 9222-4119
E-mail: robetestrich@gmail.com
www.powertoheal.net

THE BOOK THAT WILL CHANGE YOUR LIFE:

THE MIRACLE MAN

THE LIFE STORY OF JOAO DE DEUS

By Robert Pellegrino-Estrich

ISBN: 0 646 3767 X 140 pages

Is Joao a modern Christ? Read this riveting account of the greatest healing phenomenon of our time. When some people, totally paralysed, rise from their wheelchairs and the profoundly blind have their eyesight restored, when modern medicine has given up on them, one feels deeply stirred to ask some fundamental questions.

Joao de Deus puts our reality at risk, defying the certainties of medical science, forcing us to replace it with one of hope and joy.

The story of Joao de Deus shakes the bedrock of common beliefs, kindling an ancient memory that rings only too true: that with love all things are possible.

For forty-three years this extraordinary man has incorporated spiritual entities to effect healings on thousands of sick people every week. He does not charge for his services. Joao de Deus is arguably the most powerful healer of our times and must surely rank amongst the greatest of the past 2000 years.

Now in its fifth edition. Consistently voted a five star "must read" by the clients of Amazon.com this is a book that will change your life and leave you with a sense of hope for mankind

Robert Pellegrino Estrich
Rua Servidão, Qd. 20, lt. 0
Abadiânia – Goiás – Brazil. CEP 72940–000
E-mail: robertestrich@gmail.com
Tel.: + 55 62 92224119
www.johnofgod.com.au

BIBLIOGRAPHY

1   Astin, John *Why Patients Use Alternative Medicine: Results of a National Survey.* Journal of the American Medical Association, 279(1998): 1548-53

2   Vibrational Medicine. Richard Gerber, Bear and Company Press.   1988

3   Roy Stemman *Healers and Healing.* Judy Piatkus (Publishers) Ltd. London.

4   Richard Gerber, *Vibrational Medicine*, Bear and Company Press, 1988

5   Manning, Matthew, *No Faith Required*, Eikstein Publications, 1995

6   "   "   "

7   Dr Richard Gerber, *Vibrational Medicine.* Bear & Co. Press, 1988

[8]   John Ott, *Health and Light*, Ariel Press, Ohio USA, 1976

[9]   Alice Bailey, *The Tibetan-Esoteric Healing*-Lucis Press 1934.

[10] New Energy Series, John Hutchinson, 1989

[11] *Urantia Papers*, Pathways Inc. 1955

[12] David Childress, *Anti-gravity and the World Grid*, Adventures Unlimited Press, 1987

[13] David Childress, *Anti-gravity World*, , Adventures Unlimited Press, 1987

[14] Barbara Brennan, *Hands of Light*, , Bantam Books, 1988

[15] "   "   "

[16] "   "   "

[17] Robert Becker, *The Body Electric*, , Morrow & Co. 1960

[18] Harry Edwards, *Spiritual Healing*, The Healer Publishing Company, 1974

[19] *Journey of the Soul*, Theosophical Society

[20] *The Urantia Papers*. Author Unknown. 1955.

[21] *The Urantia Papers*, Author Unknown. 1955

[22] Estelle Roberts. *Fifty Years a Medium*.Corgi Books, London, 1969.

[23] Thomas Sugrue, *Edgar Casey-There is a River*. 1928

24   Alice Baily, *The Tibetan-Esoteric Healing*, Lucas Press 1934.

25   Alice Bailey *Esoteric Healing*, , Lucas Press, 1934

26   Larre,C & Rochat de la Vallee, *Rooted in Spirit—The Heart of Chinese Medicine*, Station Press,

27   Robert Becker, *The Body Electric.*, William Morris Publishing, 1985

28   Barbara Brennan, *Hands of Light*, Bantam Books, New York 1995.

29   Donna Eden, *Energy Medicine*, Putman Special Markets, New York 1998

30   Thomas Sugrue, *Edgar Cayce—There is a River.* 1928

31   H.P. Blavatsky, *The Secret Doctrine*,. Heritage Classics

32   Harry Edwards, *The Understanding and Practice of Spiritual Healing—*

33   Harry Edwards Healing Sanctuary

34   Catherine Ponder, *Dynamic Laws of Prosperity.*

35   H.P.Blavatsky, *The Secret Doctrines.* Heritage Classics.

36   Allan Kardec, *The Spirits Book*, The Brazilian Federation of Spiritism. Brazil

37   Victor Zammit, *A Lawyer Presents a Case for the Afterlife.*

38   Leslie Chytom, *The Keeper of the Flame*, Writers Club Press, 1999.

39   The Author

40

41   Barbara Brennan, *Hands of Light*, Bantam Books, 1988

42   Kyriacos, C. Markides, *Homage to the Sun. The Wisdom of the Magus of Strovolos*

43   Dr Alexander Cannon.

44   *The Universal Law of Harmony*—Theosophical Society.

45   *The Bible—Matthew 10:1*

46   Barbara Brennan, *Hands of Light*, Bantam Books, 1988.

47   Harry Edwards , *A Guide to Understanding and Practice of Spiritual Healing—*

48   Rosemary Altea, *You Own the Power*, Harper Collins.

49   Colin R. Lambert, *Healers Unlimited*, Peaceful Living Publications, Tauranga, New Zealand.

50   Joseph A. Califano. Former U.S. Secretary of Health, Education, and Welfare.

51   Dr John D. MacArthur,. *The Trouble With Tofu*, Optimal Wellness

52   William Duffy, *Sugar Blues*, Warner Books, USA

53   Rosemary Altea, *You Own the Power*, Harper Collins.